FULL ACCESSORIES OF GOD:

THE SPIRIT'S MAKEOVER

FOR

WOMEN

DeLyn Wagenknecht

NORTHWESTERN PUBLISHING HOUSE
Milwaukee, Wisconsin

Cover Illustration: iStockphoto LP
Design Team: Pam Clemons, Diane Cook, Lynda Williams

Unless otherwise indicated, Scripture quotations are from the Holy Bible, Evangelical Heritage Version® (EHV®) © 2017 Wartburg Project, Inc. All rights reserved. Used by permission.

Scripture quotations marked (NIV) are from the Holy Bible, New International Version®, NIV®. Copyright © 1973, 1978, 1984 by Biblica, Inc.™ Used by permission of Zondervan. All rights reserved worldwide. www.zondervan.com. The "NIV" and "New International Version" are trademarks registered in the United States Patent and Trademark Office by Biblica, Inc.™

All hymns, unless otherwise indicated, are taken from Christian Worship: A Lutheran Hymnal. © 1993 by Northwestern Publishing House.

Northwestern Publishing House
N16W23379 Stone Ridge Dr. Waukesha, WI 53188
www.nph.net
2020 Northwestern Publishing House
Published 2020
Printed in the United States of America
ISBN 978-0-8100-2879-1
ISBN 978-0-8100-2880-7 (e-book)

20 21 22 23 24 25 26 27 28 29   10 9 8 7 6 5 4 3 2 1

Contents

Introduction

This book was born of procrastination and was continued with love. It is meant for women and girls, so that we might learn to appreciate the uniqueness of our sex and the wonderful opportunities we are granted to share the saving grace of Jesus.

It all started with tea. Long before I arrived in California, the women of Grace Lutheran Church in Yorba Linda had been hosting wonderful ladies' teas every spring. As the tradition continued, I became involved in the planning. Over the years, as we focused on varied themes, enjoyed the company of many invited guests, and sampled amazing food, many hearts were touched. We listened to knowledgeable speakers, laughed at funny magicians, and were entertained by talented musicians. We used themes like "Patriotic Tea," "Southern Hospitali-Tea," and "Jewels in God's Crown Tea." We put on fashion shows and jewelry shows, and even modeled the vintage wedding gowns of our members. Sometimes I made food. Sometimes I decorated. Often I gave the devotion (my favorite part!).

At one tea, we set up booths of fun items that we women might like to buy—jewelry, handbags, makeup, candles, and kitchen supplies. I was slated to give the devotion but had procrastinated, probably because making scones had stressed me out. At the last moment, I walked around to the different booths and collected items from each to use as visual aids and metaphors. I talked about accessorizing our faith, and this discussion was well-received. From this devotion came the idea to feminize the full armor of God found in Ephesians 6.

Consequently, many of the stories in the devotional sections are about my friends at this fine church. They undoubtedly will see themselves reflected in these pages because they have been such an inspiration to me. I promise—I only draw on them as good examples!

This book was designed with the small-group women's Bible study concept in mind. Although it is certainly okay to read this book on your own, I believe you will gain more from it by discussing these ideas with a group of Christian sisters you enjoy and trust. Whether that group consists of a couple of people using technology to communicate across many miles or of 20 women who meet in a formal church setting, please do share your thoughts and emotions with your friends.

The six chapters (six accessories) are divided into daily readings, with questions to ponder and prayers. The six accessories are paired with six Bible sections to study. Each woman should read the five short daily entries and write her responses in the spaces provided in this book. The sixth day is designated for group discussion and reading, during which the thoughts of the individuals may be shared with the group. The ideal use of the material is in a six-week study group, meeting up with friends weekly. However, if your women's group meets just once a month, this book could be used in whatever way is best for the group. Your study could span six months rather than six weeks, or three months if two chapters are completed each month. The study also could be used at a two- or three-day retreat, with the different chapters used in several Bible study sessions spread out over the meeting time. And if you are looking for a presenter to lead the study for a women's retreat, I would be available to do that. You can contact me at delyndavis@gmail.com.

In whatever way you choose to use this book, I hope you will find it to be fun and enlightening. I hope you will come away energized with the reminder of how uniquely gifted we women are to share the love of our Lord with a world of hurting hearts.

From Desperation to Truth:

THE BELT OF BEAUTY

*"Stand, then, with the belt of truth
buckled around your waist"* (Ephesians 6:14).

Day 1

We have all felt desperate at some point in our lives, haven't we? Desperate to flee from a bad situation, desperate to fit in, desperate to be loved, desperate for security. Yet God's perfect plan for our lives takes us from desperation toward his wonderful truth.

PERSONAL MEDITATION

When have you felt desperate?

Think of some situations that became desperate because you had forgotten God's truths.

Does a situation in your life right now fill you with a sense of desperation?

Do you know someone else who is feeling desperate at this very moment?

Identify some of God's truths that ease your sense of desperation.

Consider the story of Esther. Read Esther 4:6-11 (see Esther 3–4:5 for the wider context). Think about the desperation Esther might have felt: desperation to save her people, to keep her own life, to gain an audience with the king.

> What hint do you see in Esther's response (4:11) that her trust in God's truth was wavering and that she was giving in to fear of the world around her?

> In what ways can you identify with Esther?

PRAYER SUGGESTIONS

If you are feeling desperate or know someone who is, take this time to pray and ask for God's truth to become apparent. Pray for your specific situation, no matter how small it might seem. Pray for others by name. You may also make use of the general prayer that follows.

> *Dearest Father, thank you for the truth of your love and for pointing me to that truth in your Word. Help me in my times of desperation to hold on to your truth and not to my fears. Help my friends or family members who are hurting or feeling desperate. Enable me to show them your truth, and remind me that I can be your voice of truth even in an untruthful world. Forgive me for the times that I have held on to my desperate feelings and refused to give myself to you. Forgive me for the times I have failed to share your truth with others. You are the great truth of my life, and I praise you. I pray in the name of your Son, Jesus. Amen.* ⊰⊱

Day 2

READING

Truth—what a beautiful word. What a blessing it is to know the truth! In John 18:38, Pontius Pilate asked the question of Jesus, "What is truth?" as a rhetorical question. Yet Pilate was desperate for an answer as he dealt with the mob who wanted Jesus dead. If Pilate had wanted an answer, he would have had it. We have it, don't we? Jesus himself is the Truth, the ultimate truth in whom we can put our trust.

So, Paul tells the Ephesians to "stand firm then, with the belt of truth buckled around your waist" (6:14 NIV). The Ephesians would have been familiar with the Roman soldier's belt that protected his midsection and thighs, so they understood that this belt meant protection.

As modern women, we might think of belts as more of a fashion accessory, something to make us look pretty. The truth of Jesus is both; it is a beautiful protection that we should wear every day.

My husband enjoys watching the television show *Cops*. Although I don't share his enthusiasm for the show, I remember laughing hysterically at one episode in particular. A young man was trying to run away from a police officer. I don't remember what he had done, but he was running as fast as he could with the policeman in pursuit. He was desperate for escape. The trouble was, he was wearing saggy, baggy jeans that fell below his boxer shorts, and he was trying to hold them up with one hand while swinging the other arm for increased speed. As he ran, his pants fell down around his ankles, and he tripped, falling to the ground. He was quickly captured and taken to jail. If only he'd been wearing a belt, he might have escaped or at least not looked so silly when he was taken into custody on national television.

Just like that young man, we are all criminals, guilty of sin—guilty of sins we understand, sins of which we are unaware, and sins we don't want to admit—sins that make us desperate. We are also being pursued, not by policemen, but by two distinct individuals—one who means us harm, and one who works in every circumstance for our good.

Our first pursuer is the devil, the father of lies (John 8:44), who wanders around "like a roaring lion, looking for someone to devour" (1 Peter 5:8). His ample teeth are dripping with sharp and dangerous falsehoods. Our belief in his untruths is like a pair of saggy jeans that trip us up as we run. They threaten to make us fall deeper into sin and deeper into despair. They can make us a laughingstock and become a real detriment to our testimony when we try to share our faith with others.

Satan's first lie is that we are good enough. We are good enough to earn heaven on our own merit, so we do not need a savior. He tells us it is acceptable to walk around with our spiritual pants drooping, with our "I Heart Myself" boxers out there for the world to see. He wants us to believe that we won't be tripped up.

"I Heart Myself." You see the message everywhere—on coffee mugs and T-shirts. And that's a good idea, isn't it? How can you love others if you don't love yourself? That is what society tells us on a daily basis. The real truth, however, is that we can't love ourselves or others properly without first recognizing Christ's amazing love for us.

Satan says, "You went to church on Christmas Eve; you donated your time to the homeless shelter; you're a good mom, a good wife, a good worker, a good person, a good student. Of course you're good enough for heaven. Love yourself. Depend on yourself. Take time for you. Follow your heart!" Oh, those words! We hear them everywhere. But why would I want to follow my heart of sin that so often leads me away from God's heart of love?

The lies echo in our brains: *"You don't gossip the way she does; you didn't live with your husband before you married him; you are not a thief or a murderer or a child abuser; you rarely cheat on a test or on your taxes; you almost never call in sick when you aren't really sick; your lies are little white lies—you have the best of intentions. Do you really need Jesus? Surely, the good you do far outweighs the bad, and a loving God would not send you to hell. You have done good things; you are a better person than many of those around you, and you will be rewarded for your actions."*

The devil pursues us relentlessly with these lies, and we often find ourselves ill-equipped to flee because we are not girding ourselves with the truth. Suddenly, he has us. We begin to think that our salvation comes through Jesus' work combined with the good works we do. So we work a little harder. Finally, we are no longer focusing on Jesus for our eternal good; instead, we are focusing on ourselves, certain that we are good enough, when we most certainly are not. In Romans 3:23, we read the truth—and the truth is radically different than Satan's lies: "All have sinned and fall short of the glory of God." Isaiah 64:6 tells us that our so-called righteous acts are nothing but "a filthy cloth."

How easy it is to sweep our little sins under the rug and assume that they don't need forgiveness. How many times have I been the life of the party at someone else's expense, saying and doing things that others may find amusing but that are not right in the sight of God? I console myself, and others encourage me, with words like, "This is how God made you. That's just who you are. You are fun. You are interesting."

The Christian "pants" with which Jesus so graciously clothed me, for we believers are all clothed in his righteousness (Isaiah 61:10), slip down below those silly boxers the world likes to show off. "I Heart Myself." I fall. We fall. We need to put on our belts of truth, to be reminded over and over again, "God so loved the world that he gave his only-begotten Son, that whoever believes in him shall not perish, but have eternal life" (John 3:16). This is the truth!

PERSONAL MEDITATION

What does it mean to you to be clothed in the righteousness that Jesus provided?

What sins tempt you to love yourself more than God?

PRAYER SUGGESTIONS

Confess your sins of putting yourself before God. Thank him for his robe of righteousness. Or use the following prayer:

Dear Jesus, you loved me, lived a perfect life for me, and died in my place that I might wear your robe of righteousness. Forgive me for the times I have thought of myself as one who did not need your forgiveness. Help me continue to wear my beautiful belt of truth so that I will not be tripped up by Satan's lies. Amen. ❦

Day 3

READING

Even when, by the grace of God, we do understand the incredible depth of our sin and the utter necessity we have for Jesus, Satan still has lies for us. He tries the new tack of lying about forgiveness. He throws our sin at our feet, attempting to trip us up.

"Oh my," he says. "Yes, God is forgiving—but that sin? That sin was too much even for Jesus. You are too despicable for him. You might as well just stick with me."

We listen; we fall; it hurts. Our spiritual pants slip down exposing brand new "Does Jesus really love me?" boxers.

I have a big mouth. At too many times in my life, my words have hurt someone else so deeply that I felt my shame like an aching in my bones, a churning in my stomach. Even as I asked forgiveness from the person I offended, I wondered what my reaction would be if I were wearing her pants. Was what I had done unforgivable? Other times, I have hurt someone so deeply that my sin was too much to forgive, at least for a mere mortal. Friendships were shattered. There was pain all around.

The evil one would tell me that Jesus couldn't forgive me either. How many of us feel, at some time or another in our lives, that our accuser may just be right? The Bible gives us a whole list of sins that can keep us out of heaven. My lies, my addictions, my sexual immorality—are they too much to forgive?

Is it all over for me if I had sex before marriage, if I had an abortion, if I am addicted to drugs or alcohol or food, if I have hated my parents or my spouse? Is heaven closed to me?

We often see this technique of Satan in the Bible stories we hear and read. Peter denied Jesus three times, just as Jesus had said he would. Judas betrayed Jesus with a kiss, just as Jesus had said he would. Both men had committed grave sins, and both felt the guilt of their actions. The difference was that Peter wore the beautiful belt of the truth. All Jesus had to do was look at Peter. Peter knew not only that he had been wrong but, more important, that he had been forgiven.

Judas, on the contrary, was lost in despair. He did not don the belt of truth. He focused only on the horrible deed he had done. He tried to make amends by giving back the money he had been paid and by confessing his sin. But he never thought to look toward Jesus, the Truth, his only hope. He refused to see the truth that this very Jesus whom he had betrayed was the Christ and that his death had paid for all of our sins, even for Judas' horrible act of betrayal.

Satan does a good job of spreading lies about our sin and about our Savior, and he has incredible energy to pursue us. He wants to take away our truth and lead us to despair.

Thank God we have another pursuer. Like that policeman who chased, caught, and placed handcuffs on that young man in the television show, the Holy Spirit chases after us—but his motivation is love. Sometimes he has to knock us down to get our attention. He lets us endure hardships and tackles us with trials. But when he has us, he equips us with belts of beauty. Truth after truth about the depth of God's love is revealed to us each time he tackles us and brings us to our knees. How wonderful it is to be adorned with his truth.

The beauty of his message is that God's truth, not Satan's lies, governs our earthly and our eternal lives.

A most practical accessory, his truth is a reversible belt; it has two sides. The first side is the fact that we are not good enough on our own to merit eternal life and, therefore, we need a savior to make us right with God. The second is that every sin, no matter how grave we think it is, is completely atoned for through Christ's perfect life and innocent death on our behalf. Believing the devil's lies rather than God's truth is like taking off the Holy Spirit's belt and throwing it back at him. If we do this, our spiritual pants will fall down, and the shame of our sin will be exposed. If we throw that truth back to God too many times, we show that we don't want the clothing of Christ, we don't want righteousness, and we don't want heaven.

PERSONAL MEDITATION

What sins does Satan keep throwing back at you again and again to knock you down with guilt?

What situations has God used in your life to bring you to your knees so that he could lift you up?

PRAYER SUGGESTIONS

Thank God for his forgiveness for specific sins and ask him to help you let those sins go. Or use the following prayer:

Forbid it, Lord, that I should want to throw away the truth of your forgiveness. Help me to understand that your love is strong enough to forgive all sin and that I should hand all my guilt and sorrow over to you. Amen. ✣

Day 4

READING

The beauty of the belt of truth is that it not only keeps us from falling down but also keeps us from acting foolishly. It keeps us from looking silly when we say we are Christians, when we try to present our faith to others. It is an essential piece of our Christian accessory package.

My friend and I were once discussing the purchase of jeans. What should our mom jeans look like? Do we look good in skinny jeans, distressed jeans, low-rise jeans? I told her I rather liked the comfort of the low-rise variety, to which she responded that I should not purchase them too low because she vaguely remembered seeing a bit too much of my backside on occasion. Well, haven't we all? Haven't we all turned away, not wanting to look, but afraid to tell our friend or our daughters or our friend's daughter or a stranger that her low-rise jeans have not risen high enough and that we can see parts of her that should not be available for public viewing? Maybe we were seated behind her in church or at the school play or in the baseball bleachers, and there it was, the reason many older women consider low-rise jeans to be a very bad idea. Alas, your own back side, just like mine, may have peeked out from those jeans that some dear friend should have talked you out of buying.

Low-rise jeans were all the rage for a while, but often we wearers show more of ourselves or of our undergarments than we had planned, all in the name of the latest fashion.

Enter the belt. Belts help. More than just a decoration, more than just another adornment, these are accessories with a purpose, perhaps the ultimate useful ornament. Okay, maybe belts are not *that* great, but they are pretty good. They do make it easier for us to show only our best and not the parts of us we wish to conceal. With the right belt, we won't be caught with our pants too low.

The truth of Christ that we have been taught is the belt that holds up the pants of our faith. Paul warns the Ephesians to watch out for false prophets. False doctrine, like low-rise jeans, is all the rage. We read it in books, and we see it on the screen. Its message is all over the internet, and sadly even in Christian churches. If we do not know the truth of the gospel, we are likely to be led astray. 1 Thessalonians 5:21 tells us to "test everything." Paul tells the Galatians, and through them all believers, to watch out for "a different gospel, which is really not another gospel at all" (Galatians 1:6,7). We are given all the truth we need in the Bible, the Word of God, and we need to watch out for people who try to give us their versions of the truth, which are not gospel at all.

We are asked to believe the experts, the preachers we see on the screen, the spiritual books we read. It is "cool" and fashionable to be *spiritual* but not so cool to be a Bible-believing Christian. Sometimes it is hard to know what or whom to believe.

Just like low-rise jeans, false doctrine can be comfortable. Attending a church that focuses only on God's love and not his righteousness and judgment may send us out with a smile, but our focus is all wrong. "Oh, it's so nice to know God loves me. Now, I can continue to follow my own desires because even though nobody is perfect, God loves us anyway." When we lose sight of the fact that we need Jesus and his truth, we lose our spiritual pants.

It can be comfortable to think that we are able to do something for ourselves to merit heaven. Some spiritual leaders try to convince us that we must do something to be saved. Say these words; perform these actions. God took the first step in sending Jesus; now you must take a step toward him.

But God's Word reminds us: "It is by grace you have been saved, through faith—and this is not from yourselves, it is the gift of God—not by works, so that no one can boast" (Ephesians 2:8,9).

Although the false doctrines that swirl around us are obviously not consistent with biblical truth, they are appealing to our human nature. It is so easy to fall prey to a lie. The best form of protection is to know the truth so well that we will not be led astray, so that our faith stays firmly planted in Jesus and only in Jesus.

PERSONAL MEDITATION

Can you think of a time when you professed your faith but felt ineffective because you were confused about the truth of your faith?

What points of doctrine confuse you or make you feel like you're not sure of the truth? (If there is something specific that confuses you, bring that concern to your pastor.)

How can you become more confident in your Christian belief?

PRAYER SUGGESTIONS

Ask God to help you see the truth and to overcome your areas of confusion. You may also use the following prayer:

Holy Spirit, you are the giver of faith, the one who bestows truth. Thank you for bringing me to faith in Jesus as my Savior. Help me hold on to the truth and overcome my doubts through you. Amen. ❧

Day 5

READING

Where do I find this beautiful belt of truth, this instrument that will keep me from foolishness, that will keep me from harm? I find it in my study of the Word of God.

A teenager in our congregation told me and several other adults, "I don't like coming to Bible study." The teen followed with a question, "Why do I need to?"

One clever woman answered in this way: "If I baked you a tray of brownies, and I only put a little poison in it, would you want to eat them?"

The teen answered, "No. What does that have to do with Bible study?"

"Everywhere you go, people are offering you religion, spirituality—beliefs of some kind. Some of it may taste good, but if it is laced with poison—well, you know what could happen."

"I still don't get it."

"How do you know poison when you see it? How do you know the truth when you hear it? Coming to Bible study here, where you know you can trust what you are being taught and where you are encouraged to test each doctrine you hear by reading your Bible, will help you recognize the poison that might make the brownie bad for you."

"Oh."

I'm not sure the teen got the point, but I did. This lady makes tasty brownies, but the gospel truth is more delectable than a dozen trays of her brownies. Why would we want to contaminate it with lies? "A little yeast works through the whole batch" (Galatians 5:9).

As Christian women, we need to keep putting on the truth. We can find our belts of truth in many places. For one, we find them in Bible study. We really need the belt of truth we find when we study the Bible at church or in a home where the leader is trained and experienced to answer all our questions.

It is essential that we worship with fellow believers as well, sharing in the sacraments that assure us of our salvation and strengthen our faith. Hebrews 10:24,25 gives us a strong admonition in this regard: "Let us also consider carefully how to spur each other on to love and good works. Let us not neglect meeting together, as some have the habit of doing. Rather, let us encourage each other, and all the more as you see the Day approaching."

How important it is, also, that we take time at home to read devotions and our Bibles and to spend time in prayer, asking the Holy Spirit to help us discern the truth. Many spiritual teachers tell us to meditate to achieve peace, but their brand of meditation turns our attention inward and focuses on our own strengths. The Bible too tells us to meditate—not on ourselves, but rather, on the steadfast promises of God. Psalm 119:148 provides an example for us: "My eyes look forward to the night watches when I can meditate on your sayings." This is how we put on the belt of truth to keep from being tripped up by Satan's lies or looking like hypocrites.

Truth is strong, and truth hides my underwear. Truth is beautiful.

Just as the right belt can dress up an outfit, the belt of truth dresses up our frail human selves so we are able to share our faith with our friends—we are able to love in this very special and powerful way. And this love is a beautiful love! No tripping—because we know the truth. No backsides showing—because we know the truth. I can look at a nonbelieving friend, look her right in the eyes, show her my belt of truth, and tell of its immeasurable worth to me. The Holy Spirit will help many people just like us to see the beauty in the belt of truth and desire to add this belt to the wardrobes of their lives.

Are you wearing your belt? Is it the strong, beautiful belt of the gospel truth? This stunning belt is the tool that keeps your spiritual pants where they belong. Don't lose your pants! Put the truth to work in your most desperate moments.

In difficult situations, I am protected by the truth that my all-powerful God will never forsake me. In those moments when I so desperately want to fit in, the truth tells me that I am made for more than this world—more than this life. Rather, I am made to fit into God's kingdom. When I am desperate to be loved, God's word of truth tells me that Jesus loves me far more and far better than anyone on earth ever could. Finally, it is only the truth of God's love that keeps me secure. I am always safe and sound in him. "The LORD will watch to keep you from all harm. He will watch over your life. The LORD will watch over your going and your coming from now to eternity" (Psalm 121:7,8).

PERSONAL MEDITATION

What biblical promise is most special to you?

In what ways can you become better at putting on the belt of truth in your daily life?

What is your favorite way of hearing or learning the truth?

PRAYER SUGGESTIONS

Don't be afraid to pour out all your desperate thoughts to the Lord. You can begin with the following prayer:

Loving and gracious Lord, thank you for the promises in the Bible that assure me that you love me and will never leave me. Make me desperate for you, and help me to overcome all the issues of my life that could lead me to despair. Put your arms around me and comfort me with your love. Amen. ❀

Day 6

QUESTIONS FOR GROUP DISCUSSION

Take a few minutes to share some ideas that may have come to your mind as you read this past week and as you considered how this applies to your own life. Also share with each other what you experienced in your life this week. If you're comfortable, share with one another any current situations in your life that could lead you to desperation, and ask for encouragement to help you get through them.

In his famous poem, "Ode on a Grecian Urn," John Keats wrote:

When old age shall this generation waste,
Thou shalt remain, in midst of other woe
Than ours, a friend to man, to whom thou say'st,
"Beauty is truth, truth beauty,"—that is all
Ye know on earth, and all ye need to know.

Keats was talking about art, but the poem has always reminded me of God and his truths and the beauty of leaving this world behind for the better world that is to come.

What thoughts does this poem stanza generate for you?

Why is truth a source of beauty for you?

What do you think about the importance of the knowledge of the truth?

Read Esther 4:12-17.

How did Esther's attitude change from what we read earlier in the week (Esther 4:6-11)?

How did Mordecai help Esther move from a place of desperation to faith in the truth of God's protection?

How did the Jewish people assist Esther in her important task?

In what ways can the women in your group help each other as Mordecai and the others helped Esther?

Share with each other times in which God "tackled you" with trials that made you turn to him.

Relate times in which other women helped you realize God's truth in your life.

How could your church grow even better at sharing God's truth with the members of your congregation? With those outside your congregation?

PRAYER SUGGESTIONS

Develop a list of people and situations that need your prayers. Pray for friends and family who are desperate for truth. Pray for your pastor and others who share God's truth in your midst. Choose one person from your group to pray through your list, or pray around the table. You can finish with the following prayer:

We praise you, Jesus, and we thank you for being the Way, the Truth, and the Life, and for being with us in desperate times and leading us toward you. Forgive us when we listen to Satan's lies, when we put ourselves above you by believing we are good enough to merit heaven on our own, or when we hold on to the guilt of a sin that was long ago forgiven. Help us don your beautiful belt of truth. Thank you for Christian friends, for our church, and for our pastors, who help us remember all of the promises you have kept. Continue to use us to spread your truth around the world and to help each other in times of need. Amen. ❧

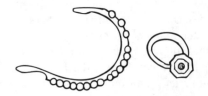

From Emptiness to Joy:
THE JEWELRY OF JOY

"With the breastplate of righteousness fastened in place"
(Ephesians 6:14).

Day 1

We women, who feel life so deeply, who desire to be someone special—to be loved, to be fulfilled—often wind up feeling empty. Our children have strayed from the hopes that we had for them; our homes are not the happy places we once envisioned. We can't find the jobs we want or the loves of our lives, or reach the goals we once set for ourselves. Emptiness hounds us, and we lack joy.

PERSONAL MEDITATION

Is there emptiness in your life? If so, what situations make you feel empty?

If you are fulfilled, does someone you know have an emptiness that needs filling? If so, how can you help?

Can you see how empty times in the past have been corrected? Or are you still feeling the same kind of emptiness you have always felt?

Consider Hannah's emptiness. Read 1 Samuel 1. Notice that Hannah has her husband's love, but his love is not enough.

What is causing her emptiness?

How was God able to bring Hannah joy?

PRAYER SUGGESTIONS

Pour out your emptiness to God the way Hannah did. No matter what is causing you to feel empty, tell your Lord. Also pray for others who are suffering emptiness. You may also use the following prayer:

Dearest God, I know that you are the One who can fill all my emptiness. I give you my pain and grief the way Hannah turned her pain and grief over to you. Help me to find joy in you. Amen. ✦

Day 2

READING

Emptiness.

Empty.

I have nothing left.

I am unfulfilled.

I have felt this so many times, and I struggle to find joy.

Where is your joy? Have you lost it amid the mundane and difficult tasks of life? Where is the exquisite jewelry the Lord gave you to wear when he brought you to faith in him? Are you wearing your joy, or is it locked away in some forgotten box? Have you let it tarnish? Do you feel joyless?

We all feel this way at some time, don't we?

During a time of great crisis in my home, a time when I was as empty as could be, a dear Christian friend reminded me to thank God for the shared joy my husband and children and I possessed. I immediately, and stupidly, wracked my brain for moments of joy I could share and cherish with my family. Marital joy. The joy of parenting. The joy of success. The joy of special times spent together. At the moment, I could find little upon which to focus. I did not sense much happiness around or in me.

My friend rightly corrected my thoughts. Our joy is not in temporal things, she explained, no matter how lovely they are. True joy is found in the knowledge that we are bound for heaven where we will praise God for eternity. This is the joy that sparkles in our lives. Even better, if this is a shared joy between husband and wife, it is a binding joy, one that remains lovely when earthly pleasures have faded or are obscured by our own sins. Therefore, we ought to adorn ourselves with joy the way we adorn ourselves with jewelry.

Jewelry makes many women quite happy. We relish the sparkle, the shine, the decoration; and although we should not begin to think that our clothing, accessories, bodies, eye color, or hairstyles are what make us beautiful in God's sight, it can be fun to enjoy these adornments. A wonderful piece of jewelry can make a simple outfit remarkable and make a woman appear put-together and confident.

Some middle-age moms like me have become too busy to worry about jewelry on an ordinary day, but many women still strive always to look their best. There was a time in my life when I spent many mornings rising before the sun to drive my daughter to skating practice. I joined a fun group of parents carrying coffee cups and offering sleepy good mornings. Many of us dragged ourselves into the rink looking rather unkempt in our sweats and ponytails, but one mom always wore nice clothing and jewelry, even at 4:30 in the morning. Whether she made the effort for herself or for others—who knows? Either way, this woman had a Christian spirit to match her jewelry. She wore her joy! She and I shared the certain hope of paradise waiting for us after this life, but I could stand to learn a few things from this put-together jewelry lady. If I take a moment each day to look to the cross and remember what Jesus earned for me there, and remember what that means for me eternally, the joy will shine like a strand of pearls. I will feel better, maybe not perfect, but better, and I will be ready to show others around me what joy really looks like. I must remember to look to Jesus for my joy, especially when I've had too little sleep and too much stress. Christ's righteousness is my joy.

I admit that I often feel too lazy to wear jewelry, and I don't always take the time to look my best. More important, though, I frequently forget to don my joy. I simply forget to look in the mirror at the child of God who is loved by Jesus.

In the same way that the right jewelry can dress up a plain outfit, joy in Christ promises to make the simplest of lives something remarkable. God's Word tells us Christians to put on our breastplates. A soldier's breastplate protects the heart and other internal organs from attacks. The metaphorical breastplate of Ephesians chapter 6 offers protection against those who seek to rob us of our faith. When in place, this practical piece of armor glistens like the finest jewelry, with joy that overshadows the ugliness of our broken lives.

When the devil tells us that God doesn't really love us, that we will always be empty, that our lives are unworthy, we shoo him away by looking in the mirror and seeing what God has made us in Christ. Then our joy begins to shine. This is a joy that lasts because we can see with clarity that Jesus will never disappoint us even if those around us do. Joy in Jesus alone prevents us from falling ever deeper into depression when we are criticized for our faith, when we fall short of our goals, and when others let us down. True joy is an irresistible sparkle that turns ordinary people into extraordinary purveyors of the love of God.

PERSONAL MEDITATION

Take a look in the mirror: What do you see? Do you see an empty shell? Do you see a woman who sparkles with joy because she is loved by God? Do you see a mixture?

Tell your reflection how much God loves her and what joy is hers to claim.

How often do you find yourself focusing on disappointment and sadness rather than on Jesus' love for you?

When others see your life, do they see the sparkle of joy?

Think of one woman you know who "wears" her joy—someone who sparkles with God's love—and thank God for her.

PRAYER SUGGESTIONS

Add your specific emotions and problems to the following prayer:

Dearest Lord Jesus, you have provided for me the gift of eternal life and communion with yourself, yet I sometimes feel empty. So many situations in my life rob me of my joy. Remind me that I am yours and you have given me Christ, my joy and my crown. Amen. ⚜

Day 3

READING

Perhaps the most difficult part of putting on joy is finding it. If I want to wear a necklace or earrings, I go to my jewelry box or borrow something from my daughters. If I need to put on joy, I have to go to God's jewelry box. Only in his Word do I find the precious ideas that I need. Every once in a while, I find myself wondering how heaven can be all I've ever desired. I've desired so much. It seems I always want more. Will it really be enough just to sit around praising God all day, all the time, forever? Why can't I just be happy now and here, where I know, or think I know, what will bring me happiness? I don't have all the details about heaven. How do I know I will be happy there?

Those times of doubt are the times when the pearls in God's book show me what a stupid, sinful human being I can be. They assure me that, yes, I will be completely fulfilled in heaven; I will love every second of being with my Lord. Reading Revelation chapter 21, I get a glimpse of what the New Jerusalem will be. Here God tells me that my tears will all be gone: "He will wipe away every tear from their eyes. There will be no more death or sorrow or crying or pain" (21:4).

I won't be thirsty either, for he offers: "To anyone who is thirsty, I will give freely from the spring of the water of life" (21:6).

I know this thirst that will be quenched is not merely a physical thirst. This is the water of life, after all. Right now, in this life, I thirst for so many things that cannot be, and I long for the gratification of dreams that should not come true—that would not be good for me. I want the kinds of earthly relationships that feel transcendent, special, perfect. Of course, these earthly connections do, and always will, fall short. I envision true fulfillment, however, in the New Jerusalem. There, a perfect life, even greater than I could now dream, will come to fruition.

Once in heaven, we will no longer stumble around in darkness wondering where we are and what is true and right: "The city does not need the sun or the moon to shine on it, because the glory of God has given it light, and the Lamb is its lamp" (Revelation 21:23). Jesus will be our lamp, not only physically but also spiritually and intellectually. We will see him as he is, and we will be his bride.

Perhaps the description that so poignantly describes the attraction of heaven for this feminine lover of precious metals and stones is found in Revelation 21:11: "It has the glory of God. Its radiance is similar to a very precious stone, like crystal-clear jasper." The chapter then lists all the incredible adornments of the city: every stone, every jewel, the gold and silver, everything lovely that exists. This is the true and lasting jewelry of joy, jewelry that will never tarnish or break. The imagery is spectacular—a city like I've never seen or even imagined. Yes, this sounds like what I want someday.

PERSONAL MEDITATION

What are some of the dreams you have had that haven't come true?

Can you think of a time when God said no to your dreams, and later you could clearly see why no was the best answer?

What is your favorite description of heaven?

PRAYER SUGGESTIONS

Thank God for his guidance in specific areas of your life. Thank him for the times he has said yes and when he has said no with the following prayer:

> *God, I see that all glory belongs to you. I know that you are perfect, and you have the ability to fill my life with meaning. Forgive me for my desires when they are not part of your will. Heal my emptiness. Show me that the plans you have for me are so much better than anything I could imagine for myself. Increase my understanding of you and my desire for you. Amen.* ✥

Day 4

READING

The trouble is, even though joy is right there in God's Word, I don't always see it and I can't always put it on. It's like the bracelet that my daughter struggles to put on by herself; she is unable to secure the clasp and needs help whenever she wants to wear it. My friend's admonition to me in my time of crisis was exactly what I needed. I was unable to find the true joy God wanted me to focus on because of all the tarnished relationships and broken clasps in my life. My friend clasped a bracelet of love onto my arm. We need to be jewelers for each other pointing to the precious pearls found in God's Word that yield lasting joy.

We need to say to each other, "Let me help you with that shiny necklace of joy, that reminder that God will never forsake you and that paradise awaits you on the other side."

A friendly reminder is all that is necessary. The Holy Spirit uses these words to soften our hearts and to dry our tears.

Sometimes a new piece of joy is given to us, like a gift, when we most need it. My husband does not shower me with jewelry and other gifts; quite frankly, we can't afford those luxuries. Once, several years back, however, he presented me with a simple but elegant emerald ring. The emerald is my birthstone. Its green hue reminds me of new life and the beauty of God's creation. That ring was a special gift that brought joy to my heart. But God gives us the most special gifts imaginable, breathtaking reminders that cause our joy as Christians to gleam even when life is at its most difficult.

Music has always been a particularly special adornment of life for me. I love not only a masterfully created musical score but also masterfully created lyrics. When I experience one of those moving, musical moments of life, I feel I have been given a glimpse of heaven, a gift from God like a diamond ring. The first time I heard the Wisconsin Lutheran Seminary chorus sing "Lord, When Your Glory I Shall See" was a moment like that when I felt that the Holy Spirit was truly giving me a picture of eternity. The words so beautifully express what will happen when I die. I tell my husband frequently that I want that song sung at my funeral so everyone present will know what I'm doing at that moment.

> Lord, when your glory I shall see
> And taste your kingdom's pleasure,
> Your blood my royal robe shall be,
> My joy beyond all measure!
> When I appear before your throne,
> Your righteousness shall be my crown;
> With these I need not hide me.
> And there, in garments richly wrought,
> As your own bride I shall be brought
> To stand in joy beside you.

Yes, that is the joy I need to remember, the joy I can put on every day.

During the summer of 2011, my family and I attended the WELS Conference on Worship, Music, and the Arts, and I experienced another poignant musical moment. For the closing hymn, the assembly sang "Jerusalem the Golden." But I could only listen and thank God—I was too choked up to sing. I suppose some of my emotions might have been due to the fact that my son was playing in the orchestra and I was so very proud of him. And certainly the sheer number of voices in the auditorium that day produced a sound that we don't hear in church every Sunday. Mostly, though, my emotions were awakened by the memorable melody and exquisite words that expressed perfectly the amazing love of our Lord.

> Jerusalem the golden, With milk and honey blest—
> The sight of it refreshes The weary and oppressed:
> I know not, oh, I know not What joys await us there,
> What radiancy of glory, What bliss beyond compare:

To sing the hymn unending With all the martyr throng, Amidst the halls of Zion Resounding full with song.

These moments are like diamond tiaras placed on our heads—as if we've won a beauty pageant. In comparison, the times when we listen to the church choir or play music at home may seem more like we are wearing costume jewelry, but that also can make us smile.

Maybe music isn't so special to you. Perhaps you find reminders of God's gifts and grace elsewhere.

I remember being on the vacation of a lifetime. We were visiting my brother in the Cayman Islands. I love the beach, and this beach was the best ever! On a cloudy late afternoon, as my family played games indoors, I stood alone on the sand and looked out to the water. A storm was on its way. The sky was darkening, and the high waves broke with loud crashes at my feet. There was no sign of the sun behind the gray, and the color of the sky was mirrored in the ocean. Suddenly, for one small moment in time, the sun burst through a tiny opening in the clouds, illuminating a cresting wave and the fin of a dolphin. Then, all was gray again. The image was so bright and so breathtaking—I'm certain I will never forget that fleeting moment. When my heart is gray like the sea was that day, I know that my God can give me a moment's brilliance to remind me of all he has told me about himself. I am reminded that the "universe was created by God's word" (Hebrews 11:3); that "through him everything was made" (John 1:3); that he is worthy "to receive the glory and the honor and the power" (Revelation 4:11); that "every good act of giving and every perfect gift is from above" (James 1:17); that "he counts the number of the stars. He calls them all by name" (Psalm 147:4); and that he still is in control, which he demonstrated so clearly when he stood in the boat and calmed the storm. He is able to calm the storms in my life now because he has power over life itself, which he revealed when he raised a little girl to life and demonstrated most clearly by his own empty tomb.

In so many ways, God is able to point our hearts back to his Word and his promises to find joy.

I have a friend who takes a few moments out of almost every day, and her days are quite busy, to watch the sunset from her backyard. Those sunsets give her the chance to reflect on the truth that God is in control of even her crazy life.

Regardless of our tastes, God knows us and knows what will make us smile. He knows us better than our best friends do, better than our spouses do, and better than our parents do. He loves us better too. These presents wrapped up and lovingly delivered by him help us recognize his grace and put on our joy. Look for these moments. Recognize them for the gifts that they are. Don't let them pass you by, and don't forget to give thanks for them.

PERSONAL MEDITATION

Can you recall a time in your life when a friend reminded you of the reasons for your joy?

Did you remember to thank her or him and thank God for her or him?

Is there someone in your life who could use your encouragement right now?

If so, consider contacting this friend. He or she needs to hear God's love if the heart is feeling empty.

Has there been a time in your life when something special happened and you were able to say, "I know that was you, God. Thank you"?

What are your favorite little slices of heaven and reminders of God's love?

PRAYER SUGGESTIONS

Pray by name and by situation for friends who may be struggling with feelings of emptiness. Thank God for specific moments of joy he has given you, and don't be afraid to ask him for more.

> *Loving Father, thank you for gifts of joy in my life, for moments when I can see you. Thank you for filling me up. Please fill me up now and continue to grant me those moments when I know all is well. Help others who are suffering emptiness or loneliness. Bring them what only you can give; and if it is your will, show them love through me. In Jesus' name I pray all this. Amen.* ⤞

THE FULL ACCESSORIES OF GOD

Day 5

READING

Once I've put on the jewelry of joy by dipping my hand into God's overflowing jewelry box, I become a reminder of God's love to myself and to others. My simple life seems more beautiful when I remember what is in store for me. The more lovely my life seems, the kinder I am to others, the more I smile, and the more positive I can be even in the midst of trouble.

When those around me see my shining joy, they might ask, "Where did you get that joy?" the same way I would ask, "Where did you get that wonderful new ring?"

That's when I am blessed with the opportunity to share some of those pearls of love that are the most precious gifts we can ever give or be given.

Perhaps the most exciting part of sharing this jewelry of joy is that it is so easy. If I admire my friend's ring and ask where she got it, she might tell me the name of the store. She doesn't have to know how the ring was made or why it is so pretty. I am already interested. She only needs to tell me where to find it. But what if I can't afford a ring like that? Then what? I have no ring.

We don't have to be able to explain everything about faith in Jesus. If our joy in life makes someone else interested in knowing how to procure such joy for themselves, all we have to do is point them to God's Word. The jewelry store is right there in the Bible on my table and in the sermons and Bible studies at my church—and the best part is that it is all free. We can all afford the jewelry of joy, and we also can share it so easily.

At 4:30 in the morning, I may never remember or bother to put on a necklace, a bracelet, or earrings. But even at the crack of dawn, I need to remember the jewelry of joy that Jesus earned for me on the cross. When I see that the joy of Christian sisters is fading, I can encourage them with the reminder that

36

all the shiny things of this life are dull compared with God's glory. Someday, my silly costume jewelry will be replaced by an ornate and precious crown that I will wear into eternity. 1 Peter 5:4 tells us, "When the Chief Shepherd appears, you will receive an unfading crown of glory." In the meantime, could I justify the purchase of a new piece of jewelry, you know, just to remind me of my joy? Better yet, perhaps I should daily read this passage from the Bible that is prettier than any jewelry I could buy:

> Blessed be the God and Father of our Lord Jesus Christ! By his great mercy he gave us a new birth into a living hope through the resurrection of Jesus Christ from the dead, into an inheritance that is undying, undefiled, and unfading, kept in heaven for you. Through faith you are being protected by God's power for the salvation that is ready to be revealed at the end of time.

> Because of this you rejoice very much, even though now for a little while, if necessary, you have been grieved by various kinds of trials so that the proven character of your faith—which is more valuable than gold, which passes away even though it is tested by fire—may be found to result in praise, glory, and honor when Jesus Christ is revealed.

> Though you have not seen him, you love him. Though you do not see him now, yet by believing in him, you are filled with a joy that is inexpressible and filled with glory, because you are receiving the goal of your faith, the salvation of your souls. (1 Peter 1:3-9)

PERSONAL MEDITATION

Are you wearing your joy?

How could you live your life with more joy so that others can see God's love in you and ask about it?

Think of someone you know who does not know Jesus.

How can you share your joy with her?

PRAYER SUGGESTIONS

Pray specifically for people you know who lack the joy of knowing Jesus.

Fairest Lord Jesus, you will always be the most beautiful part of my life. Help me to wear my joy so that others can see your love through me. Amen. ❧

Day 6

QUESTIONS FOR GROUP DISCUSSION

Share with each other any situations in your life that leave you feeling empty.

Consider Hannah's story together (1 Samuel 1).

What did Hannah do with her emptiness?

How can you follow Hannah's lead?

What specifically turned Hannah's emptiness into joy?

How did Hannah show her thankfulness to God?

THE FULL ACCESSORIES OF GOD

God's answer to Hannah's request was yes. How can you still be joyful if his answer to you is no or not right now?

As a group, consider this passage:

> Do not let your beauty be something outward, such as braided hair or wearing gold jewelry or fine clothes. Rather let your beauty be the hidden person of your heart—the lasting beauty of a gentle and quiet spirit, which is precious in God's sight. In fact, this is also how the holy women of the past who put their hope in God made themselves beautiful. (1 Peter 3:3-5)

Allow some women in your group to share stories of specific women in their lives who fit this passage. Try to avoid using as examples people who are in the room.

Share with the group times when God has blessed you with the gift of joy.

Share times when other Christian women have helped you don your jewelry of joy.

Make a list of ways you, as a group, can display your joy so that others will see it and want to know Jesus.

In what ways can you, as a group, help each other put on the jewelry of joy?

PRAYER SUGGESTIONS

Begin by making a list of people who need your prayers in their time of emptiness. Bring these people before the Lord.

We praise you, Lord, for your goodness, for the amazing love you show to us day after day. Help us to recognize that our joy comes from the promise of heaven and a life in communion with you. Help us to place our happiness in your hands. Forgive us for the times when we have failed to share your love with empty people around us. Help us radiate our joy so that others will see it and want to know you. Enable us to help each other by pointing to the joy that comes from you. Be with those who are empty. Fill them with peace no matter what their life situations may be. In Jesus' holy name we pray. Amen. ⚜

End by turning together to 1 Samuel 2 and reading Hannah's prayer of thanksgiving together.

From Weariness to Readiness:
THE PUMPS OF PEACE

"With the readiness that comes from the gospel of peace tied to your feet like sandals" (Ephesians 6:15).

Day 1

Life can be exhausting, can't it? We all have so many tasks to accomplish and so much to achieve. We are asked to do so much at school, at work, at home, and in our churches. Sometimes the responsibilities leave us feeling so weary we fervently long to put our feet up and rest and leave all the essential tasks to someone else. It would be so nice to stop worrying about expectations and instead to feel some peace. That kind of peace can come only from Jesus and his shoes.

PERSONAL MEDITATION

What situations in your life make you weary?

How do you cope with weariness?

What do you do to recharge?

Read John 4:1-26. Consider the Samaritan woman Jesus met at Jacob's well:

What can you see about her life from these verses?

What verses indicate that she could be quite weary?

Sin is the real problem. Explain.

In what ways does the society in which she lives contribute to the problem?

In what ways can you relate to this woman?

PRAYER SUGGESTIONS

Give God your weariness today and ask him for peace. Confess sins that may be getting in the way. Ask him for guidance in your daily decision-making.

> Dear Father who loves me, thank you for sending your dear Son to meet me in my daily life the way he met this woman at the well. Forgive me for my inadequacies. Lord, when I am tired, lift me up. Give me the living water that quenches my thirst. Amen. ✤

Day 2

READING

Sometimes, I'm just so very weary.

Tired, tired, tired!

Not sure I can go on.

Lord, help me cope!

Do you ever say these things when the world is too much for you? In the midst of the weariness of life, how are you coping? What road are you on? Where is your life headed? Are you wearing the right shoes?

Matthew tells us the road that leads to life is difficult, and the gate is narrow (7:14). But we Christian women can follow that difficult and narrow road. We have been given the means. We have been blessed with the right shoes, the shoes of peace that keep us on this narrow path to the glories of heaven. We walk the correct path, not because we have chosen it, but because the Holy Spirit has fitted us with the footwear that brings us peace. He has gifted us with these shoes through the gospel, perhaps presented to us with fanfare by our parents, with good humor and happiness by a friend, or with awe and respect by a pastor or teacher. No matter where we walk, even if we trip and fall, we know that we have the promise of heaven because we have the gospel—the gospel of peace. These shoes then equip us to carry that same gospel of peace to others.

Shoes, to women, are, well, everything—or almost everything. We need them like the flowers need the rain. Our desire for them is great, and we often are willing to forgo many other luxuries in lieu of a new pair of shoes.

The right shoes are important. If my shoes hurt my feet, the rest of my body does not function properly. If my shoes are comfortable but don't match my outfit, I don't feel right. Everything is amiss. I have no confidence, and I just want to hide. If

45

our men understood this phenomenon, perhaps they would be more tolerant of our need for a closet full of shoes. The color matters; the style matters; the size of the heel matters. We cannot comprehend owning only a few pairs of shoes. It simply would not be possible.

With God, however, we need but one pair of spiritual shoes. That is the pair that fits us to a tee. It is as old as the date of our Baptism, but it never wears out. It makes us look wonderful, and it allows us to stand when we think we have no strength left. Sometimes that pair of shoes may pinch a bit, but it always gives us confidence. With it we are ready to go.

The first thing to remember is that our shoes of peace come from the Holy Spirit. They were purchased for us by Jesus, not picked up on a whim through our own choice. And they are the perfect shoes for us.

For a long time, my daughter and I had the same size feet; we shared most of our shoes. To some moms, it might be annoying to step into the closet looking for the perfect shoes to wear with that Sunday dress and find them missing, abducted by the younger female in the house. Not to me. I loved sharing shoes with her because she has the best fashion sense, and I never shop for shoes without her. If she helps me pick out a pair of shoes, I know I won't be caught on an episode of *What Not to Wear* because she will not steer me wrong. She will not let me look frumpy (unless I want to and don't care what she thinks at the moment).

It would be comforting if we could automatically pass on our shoes of peace to our children and our friends, but peace isn't one-size-fits-all. The Holy Spirit brings us to faith his way, through the preaching of the Word and through the sacraments, and every believer's faith is her own. Only God can give us these special shoes.

As a parent, God used me to tie the gospel of peace to my children's feet when I, with my husband, brought them to be baptized when they were babies. Before they could even walk, they were ready to run the race that will someday take them to heaven. By praying with them and for them; by ensuring that they attended Sunday school, church, and confirmation classes; and by training them in the ways of their Lord, we have tried to keep those shoes snugly on their feet.

Now that my daughter is an adult, I think she trusts my spiritual knowledge as much as I trust her fashion sense. I continue striving to parent her wisely, grounding her in worship and prayer and devotions. I pray that she will keep wearing God's shoes, the shoes of peace, and that she will never want to trade them for the shoes of temporary worldly happiness.

PERSONAL MEDITATION

Who were God's instruments for tying the gospel shoes of peace to your feet?

Take the time this week to thank these people if you can.

If you are a mother or grandmother or aunt, if you are a sponsor, if any children are in your care, how can help them with their shoes of peace?

In what ways have you been tempted to trade the gospel shoes of peace for the shoes of worldly happiness?

PRAYER SUGGESTIONS

Remember to thank God for the people in your life who have helped tie the shoes of peace to your feet, and who continue to keep you pointed in the right direction, that of the narrow road.

Lord, thank you for the people in my life who show me your way and pray for me. Thank you for my wonderful shoes that lead me down your road to eternal life. Forgive me for the times I don't appreciate my shoes of peace. Help me to be ever thankful for your love and to share your love with others. Amen. ❧

Day 3

READING

Our feet need support. I know it is a challenge for my daughters to travel the road of young adulthood—their faith will survive only if they daily don the shoes God has given them. It is also a challenge for me to live in the adult world where I may be looked down on for my beliefs. Women of all ages need support.

As I write this, I'm living in southern California where women wear flip-flops all the time—summer and winter— to the beach and to church—with jeans, shorts, and fancy dresses. But flip-flops are so bad for our feet. Studies have shown that they cause pain in the bottoms of our feet because we constantly have to scrunch up our toes to keep them on. They also offer no arch support whatsoever.

Our lives can often feel like those flip-flops. Anti-Christian workplaces, public high schools and universities where teachers and fellow students bash our faith, and a government and a populace who work toward freedom from religion rather than freedom of religion all fail to offer us support for our faith.

That is why we need to spend time in God's Word and in prayer. That is why our teenagers and young adults need to go to church and Bible study and youth group even when they have a ton of homework or working many hours at a new job. That is why I need to call my Christian friends when times become difficult. Even that amusing Facebook post that reminds me that our loving God is in control no matter what is happening around us gives me peace and the support I need to stand up against the attacks of the world.

Although I can't give someone else my faith, I can offer the arch support that helps her stand. I can help carry her burdens when her feet hurt, because we all know that the pumps of peace are not always comfortable.

A large church group went on an outing to a local museum. The artwork in this museum is spread out in a number of different buildings, and the gardens around the structures are works of art themselves. We walked many miles that day, gazing at paintings and sculptures, flowers and trees, stained glass windows and furniture, musical instruments, and famous books. A lovely young woman who was part of our group had made the mistake of wearing high-heeled shoes. Although she looked great in them, they were not suitable for all the walking, and her feet hurt. Sometime during the trip, she and I decided to exchange shoes. I endured the pain for a while so she could walk pain free. It wasn't so bad; I have had many more years of experience walking in heels than she does.

I also possess many more years of life experiences than she, and I am equipped to bear her burdens. That same young woman often comes to me when life is difficult, and she has had to face many problems, some of her own making but most not at all her fault. She comes to me and opens up, and the words of worry tumble out of her mouth and land at my feet. At those times, I am ever so grateful that God has fitted my feet with the gospel of peace. Not only has he given me the ability to stand under the weight of my own issues, but he also has made my feet strong enough so that my friend can lean on me.

Younger women need to learn to bring their tired feet to the older women of the church, and older women must understand the privilege God gives them, to share "the peace that passes all understanding" with hurting young women.

"Encourage older women to be reverent in their behavior, not slanderers, not enslaved to much wine, but teachers of what is good, so that they can train the younger women to love their husbands and children, to be self-controlled, pure, busy at home, kind, and submitting to their own husbands, that the word of God might not be slandered" (Titus 2:3-5). This we are able to do when we wear the shoes of peace.

A woman in our congregation who was widowed at a fairly young age took on the task of mentoring a group of women she called her "twenty-somethings." The favorite activity of this group was a trip to the salon for a pedicure. Her pedicure gifts to them were of course generous and loving, but she had more to offer than just pretty toes. She ministered to their needs in more important ways: listening to their questions and their complaints, encouraging them with God's Word, and praying for them by name and by need. She pampered them with the love Jesus Christ had first given to her, and these women are stronger because of her love. This woman could not have been a helper unless she herself were wearing those shoes of peace.

QUESTIONS AND IDEAS FOR MEDITATION

If you are an older woman, take time now to identify at least one younger woman in your life and look for ways to support her. How can you minister to her needs?

If you are a younger woman, think of an older woman in your life whom you respect as a godly woman. Give her the gift of asking for her help and guidance.

What situations in your life right now threaten to knock you off of your footing?

Where can you go to find the support that you need?

PRAYER SUGGESTIONS

Ask God to help you with specific situations that make it difficult for you to stand firm in your faith. Hold up in prayer someone who needs your support or who has given you spiritual
support.

*Heavenly Father, through your Son, Jesus Christ, you have
fitted my feet with peace and with strength. Through the
Holy Spirit, you lead me along the narrow road of faith.
Help me to remember that the difficulties of this world do
not compare with the blessings that will be mine in heaven.
Thank you for the women who have guided and supported
me, and help me to be a support for others. Amen.* ❧

Day 4

READING

Today, let's focus on bringing the good news to those who have not heard it or have not listened to it. If we have the shoes of God's peace, we can hike for miles and miles to bring what is needed to those who are dying in their sins.

Our family loves to hike, and we usually can cover long distances without too much stress. On one August day, however, we endured a hike that did not go so well. We had set out on a ten-mile hike that started at the top of southern California's Mount Wilson. By the time we reached the bottom of the peak, I was already tired. Because I was having some health problems at the time, my energy was lacking. Because my husband's knees were bothering him, he wasn't doing much better.

With a little more than half the hike out of the way, we started to climb the trail back up again. It was not the pleasant hike we were used to; rather, it sapped all my strength and left me feeling defeated and exhausted. My pulse raced, and my toes ached. And that was before we missed a switchback and became lost. We had hiked a good distance out of the way in the blazing sun before we realized our mistake and turned around to find the path again. During those extra hours, as we walked additional miles, we had managed to drink all of our water. Having seen no one on the trail the entire day, we had already contacted a friend who said she would notify the rangers so they would look for us. How embarrassing. Seasoned hikers lost and out of water.

When the situation looked bleak, our children found strength. They located the correct path, sped up their pace, finished the hike, and came back for us, bearing the much-needed bottles of water. Once we had completed the hike and driven back down the mountain, we had to explain to the rangers that we were all okay and that our children had saved us. They had literally saved me; I would not have made it to the end of that trail without the water our children had brought back to me. Do you think I was happy to see those feet?

That's how it is when our Pumps of Peace come walking up to someone who is thirsting for the water of life. That was how it was when Jesus offered the Living Water—himself—to the woman at the well. Our feet are beautiful when we've taken the time to strap on our shoes correctly and have practiced walking around in them.

> How beautiful on the mountains
> are the feet of a herald,
> who proclaims peace,
> and preaches good news,
> who proclaims salvation,
> who says to Zion,
> "Your God is king!"
> (Isaiah 52:7)

This message of peace is what the lost people of the world need to hear, isn't it? We can perform a rescue by bringing God's good news to the mountain, to the city, to the beach on a Saturday afternoon, and to work or school on Monday morning.

And we don't have to be clever in our methods. God gives us the words to say: I know you are tired, worn out by a sinful world and your own sinful desires, but our God reigns. I know you are sad. Your relationships never seem to work out right. You feel unloved. There is so much strife all around you. God proclaims peace. He loves you already. Let me introduce you. I know you are wondering where your life is going, wondering how many trips to that tired old well you can make. I am here to bring good news. I am here to proclaim salvation. I am here to tell you where the Living Water is because our God reigns and he sent me to tell you all about it. Isn't that true friendship? Isn't that beautiful?

PERSONAL MEDITATION

Do you feel weary and weighed down?

Do you need help?

To whom can you go for help?

Who needs you right now?

Who is lost and thirsty on that mountaintop and needs you to bring the Water?

In what ways can you go out into the world and take peace with you?

How can you make sure you are ready to share the gospel message with others?

PRAYER SUGGESTIONS

If you are weary, too weary to complete your own journey much less bring peace to others, take your weariness to your loving Father right now. Pray specifically for the people in your life who need God's shoes:

> Even when I am tired, Lord, I know that you are there to give me peace and strength. Hold me up and give me the power and the courage to reach out with the gospel to those who need you. Give me the strength of your Holy Spirit. Amen. ❧

Day 5

READING

This chapter is called "The Pumps of Peace" partly because alliteration is fun, but also because pumps are distinctly feminine. The fitting of the feet that is spoken of in Ephesians chapter 6 refers to a foot covering worn by soldiers—male soldiers. They present, of course, a vivid image of our faith, but we as women are half of God's crowning creation, and we are different from men. We have distinct opportunites to share the gospel. This image of the soldier might make us think of men going forth to preach God's word as if going into battle. The world is often a battleground, but in our pumps of peace, we more likely are going off to share the gospel as if we are going to share a cup of coffee. We are not being wimpy or weak; we are using our strengths in a feminine way. We are equipped to share emotions, to talk about feelings, to open our arms to others, in ways that may not come as naturally to men. How wonderful it is that we are each given gifts that help us express God's love to others.

Another thing about pumps—even though they make us look gorgeous, they can be uncomfortable. Being a Christian woman often pinches us the way high-heeled shoes do. It is not easy to say no to gossip, to refuse a weekend trip with friends because we need to be in church, or to stick to our Christian parenting principles when others are calling us old fashioned and out of touch. It is challenging for young women to use their free time in God-pleasing ways, forgoing the immorality that others around them embrace. Sometimes we would like to kick off our shoes, let our hair down, and be just like everyone else.

This pinch can be a good thing. If it were too comfortable being a Christian, we might become overconfident and start to think that it is easy to be what God wants us to be. Feeling comfortable and strong, we would not look to Jesus for all that we need. We would not see the necessity of leaning on him. If my shoes of peace were comfortable all the time, they might end up being shoes of peace for this life only. They would not offer the peace with God that is the most important peace of all.

My daughter is a distance runner and a figure skater. For her sports, it is vital that she have the right footwear. Proper shoes help her run faster races and prevent injury. Her shoes wear out quickly, and we have to pay for new ones to keep her going. (We should have bought stock in a shoe company a long time ago!) We usually purchase these shoes at a store specifically for runners, but once we bought a slightly less expensive shoe at an outlet store. She ended up with huge blisters on her feet. Never again will I scrimp.

Jesus didn't skimp on our shoes either. He gave everything for them; he gave his life both in the living and the dying. The shoes that we wear that are fitted with the gospel of peace are vital to help us run our Christian race and to keep us from becoming injured spiritually. The grand thing is that we do not have to pay to replace them. Jesus paid for these shoes when he lived a perfect life and died on the cross—these shoes will never wear out because we are connected to the ultimate shoemaker. We have been given stock in God's forgiveness, and our shoes are always ready.

Proper figure skates are even more expensive and more important for the athlete than running shoes. They are often heat-molded to fit the skater's feet. And they cost a ton of money! To a skater, the right skates are priceless. To a Christian, the right spiritual shoes are priceless. They have been molded to our feet by the heat of trials and difficulties. They fit us; they help us perform at our best. The perfect boots and blades help a skater jump, spin, turn, and look elegant even in the midst of great exertion. God's shoes of peace help us navigate the jumps, spins, and turns of life. They give us peace even in the midst of exertion.

Put on your shoes.

Choose the shoes that offer heavenly strength rather than earthly strength.

When you are weary, remember your shoes of peace.

And listen to the words of Isaiah:

Those who wait for the LORD
will receive new strength.
They will lift up their wings and soar like eagles.
They will run and not become weary.
They will walk and not become tired. (40:31)

PERSONAL MEDITATION

Are your Christian shoes pinching you right now?

What discomforts are you facing because of your faith?

How can you combat these discomforts?

What unique opportunities for sharing your faith are available to you right now?

What can you do now to take advantage of those opportunities?

PRAYER SUGGESTIONS

Use this time to ask for God's help with specific areas of discomfort in your life.

Savior of all, give me your peace. Help me to stand even in the most difficult times of life. Forgive me for the times I have been too shy or too weak to share my faith. Show me opportunities to bring good news to others and give me the words to say. Amen. ❧

Day 6

QUESTIONS FOR GROUP DISCUSSION

Reread John 4:1-26 together and continue reading to verse 42. Discuss the change in the Samaritan woman after her encounter with Jesus:

How was her weariness turned to readiness?

What did she do with the gospel she received?

How can you follow her example?

Share with one another the ways in which you were fitted with the gospel shoes of peace, whether as babies through Baptism or through some other encounter with Christ and his Word.

Share with one another the ways in which your gospel shoes may be pinching you right now, and help each other find ways to combat that discomfort.

Brainstorm ways that the women of your group can be a comfort and support to other women in your church or in your families.

Discuss attempts you have made to reach out with the gospel and describe what those attempts were like.

Role-play with one another some conversations that you might have with those outside the church.

Consider this passage: "Let us run with patient endurance the race that is laid out for us" (Hebrews 12:1). What is the race that is marked out for you, and how can you persevere?

PRAYER SUGGESTIONS

If you feel comfortable, let each woman pour out her weariness while others support her in prayer. Let each woman pray for a specific person who needs to hear the gospel and needs support, and let each woman ask for the power of the Holy Spirit in pursuing these endeavors. You may finish with the following prayer:

O Prince of Peace, Living Water, the Way, we praise you for bringing us to faith and leading us to heaven. We thank you for fitting us with the footwear that will keep us standing strong on the narrow path throughout this difficult life. Help us hold each other up in prayer and with acts of kindness. Make us aware of our unique opportunities to bring the good news to those who are lost. Forgive us for our fear and weakness and for our desires to trade our gospel shoes for the shoes of the world. Give us rest. Replace our weariness with readiness, as you did with the Samaritan woman at Jacob's Well. Amen. ❧

4

From Doubt to Certainty:
THE FEDORA OF FAITH

*"Hold up the shield of faith,
with which you will be able to extinguish
all the flaming arrows of the Evil One"* (Ephesians 6:16).

Day 1

Remember to put on your Fedora of Faith to shield your mind from those who would seek to convince you that the world is smarter than God. The evil one sends his flaming arrows of false wisdom flying toward us at every turn. We must turn them away. When our thoughts spiral out of control, we can contain them by holding to the promises God has given us in the Bible.

PERSONAL MEDITATION

Which is more important: intellect or faith?

How smart are you?

Think of times when your sinful nature tries to get you to believe you are smarter than God.

From where do your thoughts come?

How do you keep your logic from endangering your faith?

Do you have doubts about your faith?

Do you feel guilty about those doubts?

Do you think it is okay to have doubts sometimes?

Consider Sarah. Read Genesis 18:9-15.
    Why did Sarah laugh?

    Why did Sarah doubt God?

PRAYER SUGGESTIONS

Confess specific doubts and fears to God and ask him to help you believe.

Dear Father, along with the father of the possessed boy, I confess and ask, "I do believe. Help me with my unbelief." Keep my thoughts where they need to be. I ask these things in the name of Jesus. Amen. ❧

Day 2

READING

A penny for your thoughts?

Sometimes I wonder if my thoughts are worth a penny.

So many impure thoughts.

So many doubts.

I pray the Lord to guide my thoughts and dispel my doubts.

I am the youngest child in my family, and my five older brothers are all extremely intelligent. Not one of them shares my faith, and conversations with them about Jesus often leave me feeling tense and stupid. Their earthly logic makes my head spin, and I have to go back to the Bible to remember the truth, to remember that I am not God, and that they are not God. Only God is omniscient; only God is the creator—the creator of all that is, including my brothers' great minds. I confess that I do not do the best job of presenting my Savior to my brothers. I often feel I can no longer share my faith with them, but I continue to pray, because only the Holy Spirit can change hearts and minds.

In some ways, I am glad I am not as smart as my brothers are. Great intelligence seems to put up stumbling blocks to faith. Our logic gets in the way because God's love seems foolish to man.

> For the message of the cross is foolishness to those who are perishing, but to us who are being saved, it is the power of God. In fact, it is written:
>
> I will destroy the wisdom of the wise;
> the intelligence of the intelligent
> I will bring to nothing.
>
> Where is the wise man? . . . Has God not shown that the wisdom of this world is foolish? Indeed, since the world through its wisdom did not know God, God in

> his wisdom decided to save those who believe. . . .
> because the foolishness of God is wiser than men, and
> the weakness of God is stronger than men.
> (1 Corinthians 1:18-21,25)

God created our intellects, so he hardly wants us to check our brains at the church door. He wants us to think, to be intellectual. Just look at how many times the Bible uses the words "know," "known," and "knowledge." Countless references speak of knowing God. On the contrary, we find almost no mention of "feeling" something about God. There is talk of love, but that love more often describes actions rather than feelings. Furthermore, most of these actions are God's actions and not those of his human creation. People of the world, along with many Christians, often see our faith as something to be felt, relegated to the realm of emotion rather than thought. This focus on emotion leads many unfaithful and highly intelligent people to consider our faith invalid because of the malleability and untrustworthiness of human emotion.

When Christians focus all of their attention on feeling the presence of God in the worship service, when the music in the worship service is all about our great love for God without telling our brains about the specifics of God's great love for us, and when we are told we must point to an emotional conversion story to prove to ourselves that we are saved, we are not taking God at his Word. We are not seeing the amazing work that God has done on our behalf. We become self-centered rather than God-centered.

In Colossians chapter 2, Paul expresses his great desire for the Colossians to "know" their God, not to feel their God.

> I am doing this so that their hearts may be encouraged as they are brought together in love, and into all the wealth of assurance that understanding brings, into the knowledge of the mystery of God, which is Christ. All the treasures of wisdom and knowledge are hidden in him. I say this so that no one deceives

you with persuasive speech that sounds reasonable. (Colossians 2:2-4)

We need to read these verses over and over when today's intellectuals or today's emotionalists try to deceive us—this is the hat we should wear to protect our heads. Faith in Christ holds those treasures for people like us, whether or not we are considered smart.

PERSONAL MEDITATION

Does anyone in your life lead you to feel stupid when you share your faith?

How do you deal with people who call you unintelligent for your beliefs?

Does anyone in your life criticize you for not being emotional enough about God?

What do you think is the proper balance between intellect and emotion in your worship?

PRAYER SUGGESTIONS

Continue to pray for people who consider themselves too smart to be Christians.

> *God, I know that you are the only God, that only you are omniscient. When I feel inadequate to speak of you, Lord, give me the right words. Help me never to be ashamed of you. Recapture the hearts of the people in my life who do not know you. Amen.* ✵

Day 3

READING

My son was gifted with a very high intellect, much like his uncles, but he was also given a strong faith and a heart for evangelism. He has a friend who is as smart as he is. Between conversations about mathematics and music, they often talk about God.

My son's friend says, "I want to believe, I want to have faith like you do, but I just don't. It doesn't seem logical." He asks all the tough questions and waits for answers.

My son does not try to argue. He keeps sharing the Word of God, inviting his friend to church activities, telling his friend that God is in control, that the Holy Spirit can provide him with faith, that he is doing the right thing in keeping an open mind and continuing to listen. If only I could be more like my son and not get flustered and say silly things. Maybe one has to be smart to know how to talk to smart people.

My son's actions do remind me to put on my fedora of faith every day. My hat goes on my head where my brain lives and keeps my brain from getting me into trouble. Rather than being changed by those around me, I can be the agent of change.

My hat is my statement. I can tell everyone that I am wearing a hat created by the ultimate designer. It may not be the fashion everyone else is wearing, but it looks and feels so good on me. Sometimes others see my jaunty little hat and want to try it on for size. I tell them the Holy Spirit will give them the fedoras of faith that they need.

It isn't just among our family and friends that we struggle to explain the wisdom of our Lord. Often, insults and attacks come from people who do not respect us or care about us. They hit us hard as they voice their disagreement. In today's society, we Christians constantly are attacked as being somehow less bright than those who do not believe in God. We are labeled as simpletons by politicians, university professors, journalists, and maybe even our bosses and coworkers.

The sole purpose of numerous internet bloggers is to bash religion. A phrase I often read on their posts states, "I don't need religion; I have a conscience." I often find myself wanting to correct their thinking. I long to tell them that their consciences exist only because God created them with the natural knowledge of his laws. I want to tell them that their consciences should condemn them and that Jesus is the only remedy for a guilty conscience. Then I think: What good would that do? I don't even know these people. I've decided that what I can do is read these posts occasionally so that I know where secularists are coming from. Then, I can ask God to give me the right words to say to people I do know, people who might ask me to refute these ideas because they know I am a Christian. Attacks on the internet are pervasive. I could be arguing all day long.

Attacks happen at schools as well. My daughter's high school English teacher was discussing biblical imagery in a piece of literature with her class, but she was not a Christian and did not truly understand the images. When the Christians in the class tried to clarify the meaning, she told the rest of the class that she understood it was difficult to believe that anyone could adhere to this faith. A Muslim child in the class said that Christians were weird, and the atheists all agreed. Uncomfortable moments such as these are all too commonplace in the United States, but they are quite mild when compared with the physical persecution that Christians around the world have had to face. Nevertheless, it is often a struggle for teenagers and adults alike to bear the teasing and remain faithful. Thank God for the protection that our faith brings.

What makes these assaults, large and small, bearable is that the foolishness of God is wiser than human wisdom and stronger than the uncertain teachings of humans. No matter what scientists and philosophers tell us, we have been blessed with faith. "Faith is being sure about what we hope for, being convinced about things we do not see. For by this faith the ancients were commended in Scripture. By faith we know that the universe was created by God's word, so that what is seen did not come from visible things" (Hebrews 11:1-3).

How many times over the centuries have scientific "facts" subsequently been proved wrong? The earth is flat; no, it is round. The earth is the center of the universe; no, the sun is the center of our solar system, which is only a small part of the universe.

The world may call our faith foolishness, but God is perfect and so great that no human can comprehend him. So, when we think about the wonders of this life, when we experiment, when we try to comprehend what is around us, our faith in what we know about God should be at the center of our thoughts to guide us as we interpret our findings. The Holy Spirit, who gives us faith, is stronger than the evidence the world proposes to contradict his word. It is a guarantee that any data that oppose God's omniscience and his plan of salvation eventually will be debunked. When Jesus comes again, in all his glory, no one will be able to call us stupid or misinformed or naïve. Until then, keeping our fedoras of faith firmly attached to our heads will help us endure.

PERSONAL MEDITATION

What situations in school or at work or on social media lead you to feel stupid because you rely on faith?

What can you do to dispel these feelings?

THE FULL ACCESSORIES OF GOD

Do you think it is productive to have religious arguments on social media or at work or at school?

In what situations is it beneficial to argue about your faith?

PRAYER SUGGESTIONS

Ask God for his help with your specific challenges of intellect versus faith.

Creator God, I give all glory to you and thank you for the wonderful way we humans are made, with both thoughts and emotions. When I am challenged for my faith, help me to know what to do and what to say. Keep my faith strong as only you can. I pray in Jesus' name. Amen. ❧

Day 4

READING

It is not just the intellectuals around us who can cause us problems. Doubts and sin can arise internally as well. Our sinful nature tries to convince us that we know more than God knows. We think we know what is best for us. I need that; I want this; and I know what is best.

We might think, "Certainly that job would be the best for me. Why does God continue to let me be stuck in this job I hate?"

"How could a loving God allow me to suffer, to be homeless, to be unemployed?"

"This marriage can't be the blessing that God has in mind for me. Surely he wants me to be happy. Surely it wouldn't be a grave sin if I left this man so I could be happy."

All these thoughts are revealed to be counterfeit when we take a closer look. The faith that the Holy Spirit brought to me through the Word of God keeps my intellect where it belongs—guided by my trust in the Lord and under the control of his precious Word. It keeps my emotions where they belong—guided by my trust in the Lord and under the control of his precious Word. My brain and my heart are kept and protected by my fedora of faith. With faith, I can clearly see that God never promised me happiness, contentment, and success in this life. Rather, he has promised me his love, his guidance, his support, and happiness and contentment with him forever. With this fact in mind, we can sing with the hymn writer:

Take my silver and my gold;
Not a mite would I withhold.
Take my intellect and use
Ev'ry pow'r as thou shalt choose.
("Take My Life and Let It Be," stanza 4)

Sometimes, when I am feeling doubt, it helps if I stop thinking like an adult and instead think like a child. I often have the opportunity to work in a Christian preschool, and my favorite part is singing with the children. I always try to find songs that have hand motions, so that even if the children are not completely sure of the words, they can understand what their hands are doing. When I sing and show "Jesus Loves Me," my faith is strengthened as much as that of the children.

Jesus loves me, this I know,
For the Bible tells me so.
Little ones to him belong.
They are weak, but he is strong.
Yes, Jesus loves me.
Yes, Jesus loves me.
Yes, Jesus loves me.
The Bible tells me so.
("Jesus Loves Me, This I Know," stanza 1 and refrain)

God made every part of us, including our amazing intellects. We can read, learn, experiment, and question. We have reasoning abilities that no other creatures in God's creation possess. Our brains allow us to make discoveries and solve problems. They also tend to make us arrogant. Our brilliance often leads us to depend on what we know, on what we can observe, and on what we can prove, rather than on the truth that God has given us.

Instead, our Lord would have us use our intellects in his service, recognizing that we are capable of thought only because of him.

When you were in elementary school, perhaps your teacher told you to put on your thinking cap. The phrase was a reminder to concentrate on the material being learned and to direct your thoughts toward the task at hand. It was an admonition against becoming distracted by the bright, shiny world around you.

In the same way, biblical teachers like Paul remind us to put on our faith-thinking caps so that our focus is fixed on our Lord and not on the secular world around us.

> For even though we walk in the flesh, we do not wage war in the way the sinful flesh does. Certainly, the weapons of our warfare are not those of the flesh, but weapons made powerful by God for tearing down strongholds. We tear down thoughts such as all arrogance that rises up against the knowledge of God, and we make every thought captive so that it is obedient to Christ. (2 Corinthians 10:3-5)

PERSONAL MEDITATION

What situations in your life or in the world have led you to doubt that God truly loves you?

How do you dispel those doubts?

Consider Romans 8:28: "We know that all things work together for the good of those who love God, for those who are called according to his purpose." What does this verse mean to you?

PRAYER SUGGESTIONS

Bring to God the specific situations in your life that may cause you to doubt his love for you.

> *God, I know you love me so much that you sent your Son to be the "atoning sacrifice" (1 John 2:2) for my sins. Keep my faith strong. When I doubt that you have my best interest in your heart, lead me to your Word. Amen.* ❀

Day 5

READING

As a story writer, I often find myself lost in my own little fantasy world. I put myself in my characters' places. For a time, I am my protagonist; I live his or her life. And my characters can get themselves into a load of trouble. The problem comes when I dwell on these stories for too long. Maybe you have some fantasies or wishes as well. You might picture yourself in a different situation—with a different job or family, with fame and fortune, possessing all the wonders this world has to offer. Fantasy can lead us into sin if it causes us to be ungrateful for the blessings God has bestowed on us. When I find myself wishing I were one of my characters instead of the person God wants me to be, it is time to put away the fantasy hat and don my Fedora of Faith.

The same thing can happen when we read works of fiction or watch television or listen to music. It isn't that these things are necessarily bad in themselves. It's just that if we get lost in them, we can forget that they are not real. I love literature so much I got two degrees in that field. I love how a work of fiction can lead me to feel what the characters are feeling, and through this, to better understand other people. Often a character has much to teach me and pushes me to expand my horizons.

I got my master's degree at a public university. Some of the Christians around me found it difficult to study some of the literature we read that went against their beliefs. Some of them had to make the hard decision to do something else with their lives. I never felt that way. I always felt that the works I read encouraged me to think of my faith. I could compare myself to the people in these books and know for certain that God held me in his hands—that I was different. We need to know ourselves and our faith well enough to walk away from what may harm our faith and stay close to what will strengthen our faith.

Many women love reading romance novels or watching chick flicks. They can be a fun and fluffy escape. If, however, those novels and movies lead us to despise our own husbands in favor of a fantasy life and to long for what those characters have, then it is time to walk away—and not just to walk away, but to walk toward something else. If our fantasy lives overshadow our realities, it is time to immerse ourselves in the gifts that God has given us. It is time to connect with our families and Christian friends, to say thank you to God for food, shelter, rain, and sunshine, to remember what we are and have, through him.

Put on your Fedora of Faith. Let it remind you to concentrate on God's plan for you—his creation of your incredible person, his plan to bring you to faith, and the mansion he has prepared for you in heaven. Let this cap remind you to direct your thoughts toward Jesus and his saving love and toward sharing that love with others.

When doubts assail you, remember in whom your faith rests. This is the God who has always been present among his people and has rescued them from slavery and famine and fear. This is the God who had a plan of salvation for us before we were born. He operates outside of time and space, outside of our meager understanding. He is God. Speaking as God's mouthpiece, Isaiah assures us, "For my thoughts are not your thoughts" (55:8).

God has given us faith to put on to keep our thoughts where they should be—on him.

My thoughts are worth more than mere pennies.

My faith is worth more than gold.

> Finally, brothers [and sisters], whatever is true, whatever is honorable, whatever is right, whatever is pure, whatever is lovely, whatever is commendable, if anything is excellent, and if anything is praiseworthy, think about these things. The things that you learned,

received, heard, and saw in me: Keep doing these things. And the God of peace will be with you. (Philippians 4:8,9)

PERSONAL MEDITATION

What fantasies about life could lead you away from God's realities?

Make a list of some of the special gifts God has given you. Have you taken time to thank God for these gifts?

PRAYER SUGGESTIONS

Confess to God any specific sins of thought and ask him to help you keep your thoughts focused on what is pure and lovely. Say thank you to God for the items on your "gift" list.

God, you are holy and perfect, and you love me like no one else can. Forgive me for letting my thoughts stray to things that could lead me away from you. Be with me always as I navigate this life, and help me to see that all good gifts come from you. Amen. ✺

Day 6

QUESTIONS FOR GROUP DISCUSSION

Share with one another some of your thoughts on your readings throughout the week, especially your answers to the Day 2 and Day 3 questions.

What advice can you offer one another about religious discussions with unbelievers?

Share some of the items on your lists of God's gifts to you.

Read Genesis 21:1-8 together:

Why is Sarah laughing now?

What made Sarah's doubt disappear?

How can we use Sarah as an example to dispel our own doubts?

Share with each other practical ways you have found to protect your faith.

Sing together (and don't worry about how you sound). Sing "Jesus Loves Me" with the hand motions. (If you don't know them, you can look up a YouTube video.)

You can find the lyrics and story behind the hymn "Take My Life and Let It Be" online. One possible source is www.christi-anity.com. You can also find it in the *Christian Worship: Hand-book* (Northwestern Publishing House 2002, p. 486). Have someone look it up and read the article to the group. Then try singing some of this song together.

You can probably also find a YouTube video to sing along with.

PRAYER SUGGESTIONS

Pray for specific people in your lives who are resistant to God's word.

> *Our omnipotent God, we thank you for our intellects as well as our emotions. Keep our minds safe from the fiery arrows of the devil with which he seeks to harm our faith. Give us the right words and the right times to reach the lost with your gospel message. Amen.* ⚜

5

From Blemished to Perfection:
THE SCARF OF SALVATION

"Take the helmet of salvation" (Ephesians 6:17).

Day 1

> Oh, the stain that is my life!
> Oh, the salvation that covers my stain!

PERSONAL MEDITATION

Read Luke 7:36-50. Think about the woman in this story:

What kind of woman had she been?

What did the people in her community think of her?

Why was she pouring perfume on Jesus' feet?

In what ways do you identify with this woman?

In what ways do you identify with those who criticized Jesus for accepting praise from this woman?

What are the blemishes in your life?

PRAYER SUGGESTIONS

Confess specific sins that are on your heart today and thank God for his forgiveness for these sins. Finish with the following prayer:

> Jesus, thank you for the great example of this woman who washed your feet with perfume and dried them with her hair. Help me to be more like her, seeing the overwhelming wonder of your atonement for my sin. Keep me from looking down on others because of their sins. Amen. ❦

Day 2

READING

My mother's jewelry box sits atop my dresser, filled with memories of her. Being a woman of little means, she never had jewels of any real worth. There are no diamonds or pearls, but she did enjoy some costume jewelry, often in bright colors to match her personality. An entire compartment in this box is packed with scarf pins—pink and orange, puppies and owls, metal and plastic. I think back and remember my mother wearing scarves with her dresses and using these pins to hold them in place and decorate her outfits. It was the style of the times, I suppose. Recently, scarves have come back into style, more commonly without the scarf pin.

I remember my mom saying once that a good scarf can cover a multitude of sins. As a child, I had no idea what she was talking about. I understand now. A busy mother, especially one who has a job at home and a job away from home, tends to be a tad harried and often a bit stained. It may be her morning coffee or baby spit-up, French fry grease or clay from the baseball field. I know there have been many times when I've noticed a stain on my dress after I have spent a full day wearing it at work or at church. I spill; I get spilled on; I get dirty. Often, when I try to wash the stains out of my clothing, no amount of soap will make those clothes clean again.

I remember one Easter morning when I had planned to wear a white dress to the Easter sunrise service. By the time I had dressed myself and my two sleepy little ones, we were nearly late for church. As I hurried to scoop up the kids and get them to the car, I happened to notice my reflection in the mirror. I was horrified to see a rather large stain just below my left shoulder. I did not have time to find a new dress in my closet, but I did have time to pull out a floral scarf and tie it loosely around my neck, arranging it perfectly to cover that stain.

87

My mother wasn't just good at dressing up, she was also pretty good at quoting the Bible, especially when she knew we children needed to hear it. She knew her statement about her scarf also applied to God's love and forgiveness. Our lives are like that white dress I put on for the Easter Sunday service, stained with sins and embarrassing. What's worse is that there is nothing we can do to clean ourselves. When a righteous God looks at us, all he sees is filth. All he sees are the stains that our sins bring. The stains of immorality, of gossip, of envy, and of hatred all leave us ugly and ashamed. We are afraid to step out in front of God and the world all stained and ugly because we know the punishment we deserve.

Jesus changed all that by covering those stained clothes with his own clothes—clothes of the purest white. He lived a sinless life as our substitute—no stain, no blemish. He died as our substitute to wash away the stain of our sin with his own blood. With his resurrection, he purchased for us brand-new garments—his own scarves of white. Now, when a just God looks at us, he sees our scarves and not our stains. He sees purity, cleanliness, and perfection.

When I looked in the mirror that Easter Sunday morning, I saw dirt. After I draped my scarf, I was ready to celebrate the resurrection of my Lord and thank him for covering my dirt.

PERSONAL MEDITATION

Think of your mother:

What part did she play in your learning about Jesus and his love for you?

In what ways would you consider her beautiful or talented?

If your mother didn't teach you about Jesus, who did?

What makes you feel beautiful?

If you are a mother, in what simple ways can you show your children how special the forgiveness Jesus gives us is to you?

PRAYER SUGGESTIONS

Ask God to help you understand the gravity of your sin, and thank him for the specific ways in which he has loved you and forgiven you.

> *Dearest Jesus, you have covered over all my blemishes with your righteousness. I know that I am able to love only because you loved me first. Amen.* ❦

Day 3

READING

Some say that scarves are not their style. Their clothing is a reflection of who they are, and they just are not "scarf people." That's okay; what we wear should reflect our tastes. Those who scorn the scarf of salvation because it cramps their style, however, will receive exactly what their sins demand. How many friends do we have or people do we know who are morally fashionable like the Pharisee in our Bible story? They volunteer; they donate; they care; they are good people. But if we mention Christ's sacrifice for us, they do not want to claim it. "Christianity is fine for you," they say, "but I'm just not a Jesus kind of person. Let's agree to disagree; let's coexist happily."

Of course, we can't force our friends to believe in Jesus as their Savior any more than we can force them to wear scarves, but we also can't pretend that all religions are the same and are equally capable of saving us. Like it or not, the people we love need those scarves of salvation that only Jesus can give. Our scarves of salvation are uniquely gifted to us by Jesus who is "the Way and the Truth and the Life" (John 14:6).

It can be difficult to happily coexist when someone we care about is in danger of eternal damnation. But coexisting is fashionable, and we often end up practicing our faith in the fashionable way. It is so tempting to hide our scarves in order to get along with others, to avoid strife. We think that if we flaunt our salvation and cover our sin stains, our friends will think that we are behaving in that "holier than thou" fashion that everyone hates. Isn't it better to be tolerant and nonjudgmental? Does everyone need to know that I am a Christian? Does everyone need to see my scarf of salvation?

Bluntly put: yes.

Jesus himself said, "Whoever is ashamed of me and my words in this adulterous and sinful generation, the Son of Man will also be ashamed of him when he comes in the glory of his Father with the holy angels" (Mark 8:38).

If I think that I can't mention my faith because I am going to a secular mom's group where some people may be offended, then I am hiding my salvation. I am putting my scarf away at the back of my closet because I don't want to experience the discomfort it might cause. "I don't want this. It makes me uncomfortable. Of course, we can agree to disagree, and we can coexist."

We don't have to make it a point to talk about Jesus every second of every day and in every circumstance. The truth is that if we are studying God's word and we understand without a doubt what Jesus has done for us, our scarves of salvation will be visible without us ever flaunting our faith. Notice the woman in the Bible story. She wasn't expecting anyone else to worship Jesus. She did not force anyone else to help her wash his feet. But she was not afraid to show her love and gratitude no matter who was watching and judging. She had been forgiven so much that her thankfulness overflowed without shame.

We can and should remember our faith at all times, treating the people around us with love and respect and in other ways letting our actions flow from and reflect our faith. I can go to that playdate and be kind, peaceful, and humble. I can avoid participating in gossip. I can stand up for my faith if it is challenged and be prepared to share my faith if anyone wants to know. In short, I need not use my scarf to hide myself from others or to bind up others in their sins. Rather, I will wear my scarf happily and gratefully like a bride wearing her wedding dress. Can you imagine wanting to hide your wedding gown?

I will rejoice greatly in the LORD.
My soul will celebrate because of my God,
for he has clothed me in garments of salvation.
With a robe of righteousness he covered me,

like a bridegroom who wears a beautiful headdress
   like a priest,
and like a bride who adorns herself with her jewelry.
   (Isaiah 61:10)

PERSONAL MEDITATION

What situations tempt you to hide your scarf of salvation?

How can you show your faith without being overbearing?

PRAYER SUGGESTIONS

Pray for strength and boldness for those specific situations that give you anxiety about sharing your faith. Pray for those around you who need Jesus.

Dearest Jesus, you clothed me in righteousness when you paid for my sin. Thank you for your great love for me. Your love makes me want to praise you day and night. Help me to remember how beautiful and special my salvation is. Give me courage not to hide my faith but to let my light show. Amen. ✻

Day 4

READING

In addition to being fashionable and capable of covering stains, scarves are often worn for warmth. A good scarf tied around the neck protects us from chilly winter winds. Our scarf of salvation protects us from the coldness of this sinful world. How nice it is to receive a scarf like that from another person.

My husband and I were married in Florida. I had lived there my entire life, and I had never seen snow. Right after the wedding, we moved to Wisconsin. I was so cold, but I had a scarf and hat and winter coat to protect me from freezing. My scarf had been given to me by a friend in Florida as a parting gift. She knew I would need it. She had experience with the world up north and knew how cold it could be. Her scarf was a beautiful gift to me.

How much more thoughtful and caring would it be to present to someone the scarf of salvation to protect her from the dangers of our sinful world? When I was younger, I worked with a wonderful Christian woman who practiced her faith in a quiet manner, and I admired her peacefulness. I knew my Savior, but I was so caught up in a world of sin that I didn't know what to do. I was unrepentant and in danger of losing my faith. This dear lady could have slipped the noose of the law around my neck. She could have told me how horribly I was acting and what awful punishment I deserved, and she would have been right. I don't know if I would have been "scared straight" or if I would have just ignored her and thought of her as being mean.

Instead, she put aside the noose and wrapped around my neck a warm scarf of salvation. She lovingly told me that I was doing wrong and that our loving Lord did not want this to be my life. He wanted to give me abundant life instead. Rather than pretending to be holier than I, she admitted to her own guilt. I knew that she understood me and cared for me. She then spoke of Christ's unfailing love for both of us. It was as if she was saying, "Dear friend, let me wrap you in the warmth that is Jesus' sacrifice for your sins. Let his life, his death, and his resurrection keep you safe from the cold of your sinful nature."

Had it not been for the care of this woman, I might have let Satan's noose hang me in my sin. My entire life changed because God used this woman to reach me. Indeed, I changed. I repented my sinful life. I came to appreciate so much more the forgiveness that had been given me. I took to heart the many verses in the Bible that tell us that loving God means keeping his commandments. I'm still a sinful woman, but because of that lady—that instrument of God's love—my path changed. Oh, the warmth of God's love presented by one imperfect human being to another!

PERSONAL MEDITATION

Are you at this moment caught up in a sinful activity that is putting your faith in danger?

Has anyone in your life loved you enough to point out your sin and redirect your thoughts to your salvation through Jesus?

Does someone you know need you to point out her sin and redirect her to her Savior?

PRAYER SUGGESTIONS

Thank God for specific people in your life who have helped you more clearly see your salvation through Christ. Pray for specific people you know who need this reminder.

Thank you, Lord, for the loving people who have wrapped me up in your warmth and love. Fill my heart with love for those who are straying, and take away any feelings in me that I am better than those people. Instead, help me reach out to others with your love through Christ Jesus. Amen. ✢

Day 5

READING

We experience so many moments in our lives when things happen that threaten to freeze our fragile hearts. We make mistakes at work and suffer the reprimands of bosses. We argue with our spouses. We lose patience with our children. We become involved in petty arguments with other women in our church families over petty issues like what color the table-cloths should be, who should be in charge of which activities, and what hymns we wish to sing. It is a horrible feeling when the workplace is icy, our homes have become cold, and even church life feels chilly and uncomfortable.

During just such difficult times, putting on the scarf of salvation gives us hope for the future and reminds us that these earthly sufferings are so tiny compared with the sufferings of Jesus on our behalf. We remember Romans 8:18: "I conclude that our sufferings at the present time are not worth comparing with the glory that is going to be revealed to us." Wrapping ourselves in God's love warms and softens our hearts, leading us to forgive and to ask for forgiveness. We wrap ourselves up when we put on beautiful words, such as these: "God demonstrates his own love for us in this: While we were still sinners, Christ died for us" (Romans 5:8).

My boss may always be cold, and I may never be the perfect employee she wants me to be. But my scarf reminds me that Jesus loves me in spite of my faults and inadequacies, and he will never give me the cold shoulder. My scarf provides the warmth to endure chilly professional situations and the strength to continue my efforts with the hope of better success in the future.

If strained relationships at home have made for a cold family, this is the time to pass out the scarves. This is the time to remind your family members of their faith. Do you have a husband who needs to be reminded that it is his job to wrap you up in your scarf of salvation? Does he know how much you long for him to protect you and remind you of your faith? Maybe, it's time to gently remind him. Do you recognize that you are longing for that as well? Do you make it obvious that you respect him as a gift from God? Or are you running away from his leadership? Don't be afraid to willingly submit and see what God can do!

Do you have a husband or boyfriend who does not share your faith? It is time to remember that scarf. Put it on and show your faith to your husband, your boyfriend, or your father. It is time to remember who you are and to pray for the men in your life whom God has put into leadership positions—whether they are husbands, boyfriends, fathers, brothers, or leaders in your church.

Is there strife between parent and child? If you're the mom, this is the time for prayer. Pray that God will lead your children to recognize the importance of that scarf of salvation. Wear your scarf every day in front of your children. Model your faith, and guide your children, even if they don't seem to be listening. James tells us, "My brothers, if anyone among you wanders away from the truth and someone turns him back, let it be known that the one who turns a sinner from the error of his way will save his soul from death and will cover a multitude of sins" (James 5:19-20). Isn't that who we want to be for our children?

If you are a young woman who does not understand your mother in any way, remember that you share that scarf of salvation. Don't let prayer be something she does for you but that you don't do for her in return. Try not to think of that scarf as something that will hold you down and suffocate you. Try to think of it as the warm blanket she gave you to comfort you as a child.

When families see each other as children of God, dearly loved and forgiven through Jesus, when they remember to don their scarves of salvation, they can battle the cold sin together rather than battling each other.

Putting on our own scarves of salvation also leads us to recognize the scarves of others in our churches. This recognition reminds us who we all are—redeemed children of God. We are all the same, and our arguments with our sisters in Christ are arguments with ourselves, "because we are all members of one body" (Ephesians 4:25).

When I am kneeling at the communion rail next to the woman I think made a poor decision or is arrogant or doesn't care about my feelings, it is hard to remain angry. We are both on our knees in front of our Lord. We are both sinful. We are both forgiven. If God could forgive us both, how can I not forgive her and wrap that warm scarf around us both?

When nothing in my life is going right, I must wrap myself up in God. I must cling to the faith that I have been given. My faith is in the One who is almighty and who is the perfect lover of my soul. When I feel my heart freezing over, it helps to remind myself that "all things work together for the good of those who love God, for those who are called according to his purpose" (Romans 8:28).

Our scarves of salvation cover over our sins and warm our hearts. Remember to put on your scarf every day.

Stay clothed in Jesus's righteousness.

Stay warm in God's love.

PERSONAL MEDITATION

Are any of the relationships in your life strained?

In what ways can you reach out in these relationships and share the beauty of your salvation?

Do you have the courage to ask for help from your husband or boyfriend, from your parents, and from other women in your church?

How can you ask for help and how can you give help?

PRAYER SUGGESTIONS

Take this time to pray for the difficult relationships in your life, and listen for God's answers.

Father God, thank you for my scarf of salvation. Thank you for seeing Christ's righteousness when you look at me. Thank you for the warmth you provide. Forgive me for not appreciating those around me who want to guide me in my path toward a deeper understanding of you. Protect those in authority over me, and give us all your peace. Amen. ⊰

Day 6

QUESTIONS FOR GROUP DISCUSSION

Share some of your answers from this week's questions.

Share with one another stories of how other women helped wrap you up in your salvation scarf.

Reread Luke 7:37-50 together:

Who was this woman?

Why did she love Jesus so much?

She could have hidden away from the eyes of her community, knowing that they thought she was reprehensible. Why, then, was she so bold?

Why did Jesus commend her?

Do you have anything at all in common with this woman?

What can you learn from her behavior?

Consider this passage: "Above all, love each other constantly, because love covers a multitude of sins" (1 Peter 4:8):

What do these words mean to you?

How can you make this idea a reality in your church?

Consider the following passage: "Instead, be kind and compassionate to one another, forgiving one another, just as God in Christ has forgiven us. Therefore, be imitators of God as his dearly loved children. And walk in love, just as Christ loved us and gave himself for us, as a fragrant offering and sacrifice to God" (Ephesians 4:32–5:2):

How can your little group become a more fragrant offering to God?

What are some specific ways you can show love and forgiveness to one another?

How can your group find others outside of your fellowship and wrap them up in their warm salvation?

PRAYER SUGGESTIONS

Thank God for each other.

Lord, thank you above all else for your forgiveness—for washing away all our sins. Thank you for fellow believers who remind us of our salvation. Strengthen our relationships with one another and in our families. Help us to reach out with your gospel message this week. Amen. ⊹❀

From Anxiety to Confidence:
THE HANDBAG OF HAPPINESS

*"Take . . . the sword of the Spirit,
which is the word of God"*
(Ephesians 6:17).

Day 1

Sometimes, I feel so unprepared.

Sometimes, I am so unhappy.

Sometimes, I am so lost!

QUESTIONS AND THOUGHTS FOR MEDITATION

Reread the book of Ruth. When we study Ruth, we often focus on Ruth as a faithful person, a girl willing to stay with her mother-in-law even when it meant leaving everything she knew. But take a minute to think about Naomi:

Does Naomi have reason, as she packs up to head home, to be anxious?

How could having Ruth along with her increase or decrease her anxiety?

Is Naomi still anxious when she reaches her homeland? Why?

What parts of your life lead you to feel anxious and unprepared? What are you worried about?

PRAYER SUGGESTIONS

Take every anxiety to God. Don't be afraid to make a list of every worry in your life. God has time and patience to hear them all.

I am so worried about so many things in my life, Lord. Please remind me of the truth of the psalmist's words, "My times are in your hand." Give me your comfort. Prepare me through your spirit for difficult times ahead. Amen. ❧

Day 2

READING

What's in your handbag? When you look at the contents do you get the feeling you are prepared for everything? Can you meet any situation head on with only the contents of your purse? Do you carry a Handbag of Happiness?

It happens every day: My children go digging through my purse in search of money, which I rarely have, or lip balm or gum or mints, all of which I usually do have. In church every person who sits in the row with our family reaches out a hand for a mint just before the service starts on Sunday morning. Somehow, I have become everyone's mom.

It is kind of a mom thing, isn't it? "Always prepared" may sound like the Boy Scout motto, but the Boy Scouts have nothing on moms. I know moms who carry tissues, bandages, snacks, scissors, toys, wipes, sunscreen, and safety pins—they always have everything they need. Sometimes I feel a bit less organized than I should be when I don't have exactly what is needed at the moment. Those handbags are weapons in the parent war, tools that keep moms sane in the midst of parenting stress.

In our spiritual lives, we need to be prepared the same way. The sword of the Spirit from Ephesians chapter 6 is a weapon to use against spiritual enemies. In our handbags of happiness, we carry the tools and weapons that keep us safe and happy in our faith. They are tools that keep us focused on Christ. No matter where we are, our handbags should contain several essential items.

The first and most important tool is the Word of God. The Word brings us to faith. It shows us our sin and our need for a savior. It gives us the gospel message of salvation through Jesus Christ. It works in our hearts to keep our faith strong, and it gives us the courage to be a testimony to others. Although it is actually a great idea to carry around a small Bible in our actual purses, the Handbag of Happiness is a figurative bag. The way to carry around the Bible is to memorize its words and internalize its concepts. The more we know about what God says in the Bible, the better prepared we are to face criticism, to keep calm in difficult situations, and to be "prepared to give an answer to everyone who asks you to give a reason for the hope that is in you" (1 Peter 3:15).

How would I feel if I did not have any mints in my purse on Sunday mornings when all those hands were reaching out to me? I would feel as though I were letting everyone down. It is much nicer to feel prepared and to see people smile. How much worse would I feel if I couldn't tell someone about Jesus when their hands were outstretched? And oh, how much better would be the feeling of giving someone the life-saving Word of God. So, I replenish my purse with mints, and I replenish my soul with the knowledge of God's saving grace through Jesus Christ. That way, I am always prepared, and that handbag of happiness makes others as happy as it makes me.

I am reminded of two amazing autobiographies I have read. In each case, for the women telling their stories, a Bible was literally the only thing that kept them going. The prized possession, the Word of God, was worth more than food and clothing or the prospect of escaping physical pain. It was the one thing they desired and the only thing that gave them hope. God revealed his glory to both of these women by providing miracles for them.

The first book is *The Hiding Place*, the story of Corrie ten Boom. Corrie and her sister used their Bible, smuggled into a Nazi concentration camp, not only to comfort themselves but also to proclaim Jesus and his love to their fellow prisoners. The other book is entitled *Left to Tell: Discovering God Amidst the Rwandan Holocaust*. It is the story of Immaculée Ilibagiza, who was hidden in a bathroom with a group of other women for months, her Bible the saving grace of her life. I read these stories, and I wonder how I can learn to value God's Word as

107

these women did. I marvel that in this time of extreme per-secution and fear God so imbued their hearts with such love and devotion. He protected the souls of his own dear creatures through his Word.

God lovingly protects my soul as well, and books like these so clearly remind me of this truth. The power of his Word and his love is thrust before my eyes in a way that is impossible to ignore whenever I read these stories, and whenever I read the stories of the heroes of faith generously presented for us in the Bible. I pray that God will give me this kind of love for and devotion to his Word.

Even if I never find myself in such frightening circum-stance like those Corrie ten Boom endured, in which I would need the Word of God to survive, I can still take it with me wherever I go. The more verses I have memorized, the more I will be able to recite when I am feeling anxious or afraid, and the more peace the Holy Spirit will be able to bring to my heart.

A friend of mine recently had to be perfectly still for an extended period during an MRI exam. To calm her anxiety, she recited Bible verses and played back in her mind the song she had heard the choir sing in church on the previous Sunday, a song that was filled with gospel comfort. Taking God's Word with us wherever we go will bring us confidence and calm our hearts as we face our fears.

PERSONAL MEDITATION

What Biblical heroes or stories of faith are most important to you and give you inspiration and strength?

What steps can you take on a daily basis to keep God's Word at your fingertips?

To what degree do you find strength in devotional books and in online devotions?

Are you able to discuss God's Word with your friends?

How can you adjust your schedule to make time in God's Word a priority?

Do you need to rise earlier?

Do you need to cut something else, like some television or social media time, out of your life?

How can you include your children in your Bible time?

PRAYER SUGGESTIONS

Thank God for specific heroes of faith that inspire you to keep his Word in your life.

Lord, Psalm 119:105 tells me, "Your words are a lamp for my feet and a light for my path." Never let me forget that your Word is essential in my life. Holy Spirit, help me to love you and your Word above all else. Amen. ❧

Day 3

READING

The second essential tool to put in our handbags of happiness is the use of the Sacrament of Communion. In my purse, I might carry a snack, especially if I have a long day of meetings that might sap my strength. I also carry snacks for my teenagers. They are bottomless pits, hungry every second of every day, always needing sustenance for schoolwork, sports, and other pursuits. After a ten-mile run, my daughter always wants me to bring her water, a sports drink, and food. On a daily basis, she eats tons of lean protein and mounds of vegetables. On the day before a race, we load up on carbohydrates.

Isn't that the way we are as Christians? Living our day-to-day lives weakens us and makes us hunger and thirst for the promises of our Lord. We are better able to live our lives with confidence and power when we are fed. We can persevere through the challenging marathons we must face if we are properly nourished.

Once our family went for an oceanside hike at dusk. We trekked up and down hills and watched the full moon rise above us. It was a long hike, so we decided to stop on the way home for food. We just ate hamburgers and milk shakes, but those were the best hamburgers. I really appreciated that food.

Do I appreciate the Lord's Supper that much? For many, I think Communion has become just something that happens during the worship service. I've even caught myself thinking, "Oh, I wish it weren't a Communion Sunday. Communion always makes the service so long!" Many of us think of the music as the best part of the service, and many think the sermon is the most important part. Certainly, the gospel in the sermon and the gospel in the hymns, songs, and liturgy are important, but so is Communion. It is the one place in the service during which God physically touches us.

One woman in our congregation values Communion so much that she will call the pastor and ask if he can stop by her house or if she can come to his office to receive private Communion between times that it is offered during the worship service. She needs that physical assurance of her faith, and the pastor is always happy to accommodate.

Once, a friend's husband had been absent from worship for a while. His life at the time was a struggle, and we had prayed together for him and for his faith. When he came back to church, I watched from my seat as the couple knelt together at the altar to receive the body and blood together. I became quite emotional and could not hide my tears. People around me wondered what was going on, but my friend knew. When she walked back to her seat, she gave me a knowing smile. Our prayers had been answered!

What an amazing gift the Lord's Supper is for us. The body and blood of Christ conveys the gospel, which is essential to our salvation. They visibly and tactilely connect us to God's love for us. This feast is such an intimate way for God to assure us of our forgiveness. Imagine the love that was poured out for us on that cross—taste it and feel it!

PERSONAL MEDITATION

Think about what the Lord's Supper means to you.

Could you explain Holy Communion to someone who has not experienced it?

If you need help understanding the Lord's Supper, try reading *Lord's Supper: The Lamb's High Feast* (2007) by Arnold J. Koelpin. It is part of the People's Bible Teachings series, published by Northwestern Publishing House.

Has there been a time when the Lord's Supper was particularly special to you?

PRAYER SUGGESTIONS

Thank God for your church family, and ask him to strengthen it.

Thank you, loving Lord, for the gift of Communion that I can share with my fellow believers. Through this holy meal, help me to know your love. Increase my appreciation of the sacrament. Amen. ⚜

Day 4

READING

The third terrific tool we can carry in our handbags of happiness is the tool of communication—communication with fellow Christians and communication with God. One important item every woman carries in her purse is her cell phone. I know women who can't last five minutes without texting, checking email, or tweeting something on their smart phones. They depend on their phones for directions to help them find where they are going, for the latest news, and, most important, to keep in contact with friends and family.

Although many people think cell phone usage has become a prevalent problem, maybe even an addiction, my cell phone has guarded me from sin and has been a tool to strengthen my faith. One Valentine's Day, my husband did not do what I had expected or hoped that he would do. I was hurt and angry and was falling into sin. I sent off a text to a dear friend; it contained some not-so-nice words about the love of my life. She answered right away, and her answer was just what I needed. She reminded me of some important facts about a marriage between two Christian people. She calmed me down, or more accurately, God calmed me through her—I was able to appreciate my husband and refrain from saying hurtful things to him.

Talking with Christian friends, especially our female friends, keeps us strong. Communication with true Christian friends, who are available to share our victories and defeats, our happiness and sorrow, words of admonition and words of forgiveness, is among the most amazing blessings we have.

We were not meant to be alone in our faith. I should not wallow in my misery or keep my happiness to myself. I should not, however, seek the advice and solace of someone who does not believe as I do. Of course, I have friends who are not Christians. We all do. We can enjoy their company, respect them, love them, and share the gospel with them. But when troubles arise, we should not look to them for the help we need. They probably will tell us what we want to hear, but they also might steer us away from God. Our Christian friends, however, will be able to share the wisdom that is rooted in the gospel.

I once had a friend who was feeling unhappy in her marriage; she was afraid she was losing her identity. A secular counselor had told her to leave her husband and search for what she needed. She assumed that a God who loved her would want her to be happy rather than to stay in a marriage that made her sad. She thought that she would be a better Christian and a better mother if she were away from her husband and hence a happier person. She was not being abused; they just didn't have a happy marriage.

Her Christian friends reminded her of what God says in his Word about marriage, and they all offered their support and help. They told her that God promises his love and an eternity with him, but he does not necessarily promise happiness in this life. They told her that God is capable of making her husband the man that she needed him to be. They told her that her marriage vows were sacred and that leaving her husband would be wrong. Her pastor, of course, had the same message. But something about hearing this message from other women—women who may have felt what she was feeling—made it easier for her to hear. In the end, she stayed with her husband, and they are still together. I don't know if they are happy, but maybe they are content. A special kind of contentment comes from entrusting our lives to the hands of God. When we do that, God often blesses us with happiness. Communication with the right people kept this friend—and can keep us all—from plunging down a sinful path. May we listen!

PERSONAL MEDITATION

Is there a friend you haven't talked to lately?

If so, call her to catch up.

Have you ever found it difficult to tell a friend the truth rather than what you thought she wanted to hear?

Can you think of a time when talking to a Christian friend brought you back from a dangerous place?

PRAYER SUGGESTIONS

Thank God for specific people who have helped you by saying just the right words. Ask him to use you to help others.

God, thank you for my female Christian friends. They are such a blessing in my life. Help me to be the kind of friend my friends need in their lives. Help me know the right things to say to bring my friends closer to you. Amen.

Day 5

READING

Communication with Christian friends is a terrific tool, but communication with the Almighty God is even better. The phrase "the power of prayer" has become quite the cliché in our society. Whenever something tragic occurs, what does everyone immediately say? They say, "Our thoughts and prayers go out to them." What does that even mean? In truth, in most cases, it means absolutely nothing. Yes, these are well-meaning caring people, and their sentiments are nice, but they don't really know what they are saying. Prayer is not powerful unless it is true prayer, and it is only true prayer when it is directed toward the only true God, who gives this gift of prayer to his people when they come to faith in Jesus.

In movies, when a person says, "God, I don't know if you are real, but . . . " that is not prayer. Prayer is so much more amazing than that. It is the perfect present. We lowly humans have the privilege of speaking to the Almighty, of telling him everything we feel, think, and desire. We can praise him, love him, entreat him, and pour out our hearts to him. In the midst of tragedy, joyful events, or challenges, rather than sending our prayers outward toward the person affected, our job is to send our prayers upward to God, who is the only one capable of responding, comforting, or affecting any change.

If I carry communication with God around with me everywhere I go, I will never be alone. In 1 Thessalonian 5:17, God urges me to "pray without ceasing." That often seems impossible to do, but failing to talk to God is a result of my own sin, not of his being inaccessible. He is always available and always willing to listen. I need to be reminded of this fact continually.

The last section of the book of James is all about prayer. In James 5:16, we read, "The prayer of a righteous person is able to do much because it is effective." God has the power to heal the body, the mind, and the spirit. He has the power to mend

117

relationships, to bring about peace, and to bring his children back to him. When I ask for something according to his will, he is happy to oblige. The problem for us is that he answers "according to his will." Oh, how much I want what I want instead of what God knows is best for my eternal well-being. Even so, I can talk, I can ask for what I want, and I need not be afraid of that powerful God because he is also a loving God who is eager to hear me and help.

When it feels like we do not have time to pray because our lives are too busy, we need to remember that prayer can happen in the midst of our busy days. We can talk to God while we cook. We can say a quick prayer at our desks before beginning a work task. We can even pray while we're driving, when we're walking the dog, or while changing the baby's diaper. It's like going through every day with an invisible best friend by our side and chatting about all that is happening. During these normal times, it actually can be easier to pray than it is when crisis comes.

As a person who makes a living using words and communicating with others, I am often surprised when I don't know what to say to God. This usually happens when I am distressed about a situation in my life, when I am feeling guilty about a sin, or when my heart aches because my life is not the fairy tale that I want it to be. That is why Romans 8:26 is such a special verse to me: "In the same way the Spirit helps us in our weakness. We do not know what we should pray for, but the Spirit himself intercedes for us with groans that are not expressed in words." How comforting it is to know that God knows me, yet still he does not turn away. He knows every desire of my heart. Even when there are no words, I can talk to God.

We often sing "What a Friend We Have in Jesus" in our church services. The hymn is a favorite among Christians. I have to admit that I do not enjoy singing this song; there is something about the tune that I don't like—just a matter of taste. I know my husband and children have heard me complain about singing it on a number of occasions. The words, however, do fit when thinking about prayer. This fact just shows that it is the parts of our lives that we find tedious and somewhat less than entertaining that are often the most edifying and helpful. I do love God's sense of humor.

These lyrics tell us that we need to make communication with our Lord a tool that never leaves our sides.

> What a friend we have in Jesus,
> All our sins and griefs to bear!
> What a privilege to carry
> Ev'rything to God in prayer!
> Oh, what peace we often forfeit,
> Oh, what needless pain we bear,
> All because we do not carry
> Ev'rything to God in prayer!
>
> Have we trials and temptations?
> Is there trouble anywhere?
> We should never be discouraged—
> Take it to the Lord in prayer.
> Can we find a friend so faithful
> Who will all our sorrows share?
> Jesus knows our ev'ry weakness—
> Take it to the Lord in prayer.
>
> Are we weak and heavy laden,
> Cumbered with a load of care?
> Precious Savior, still our refuge—
> Take it to the Lord in prayer.
> Do your friends despise, forsake you?
> Take it to the Lord in prayer.
> In his arms he'll take and shield you;
> You will find a solace there.
> ("What a Friend We Have in Jesus," stanzas 1-3)

Another amazing aspect of prayer is that we can do it in a group. Not only is God listening to me as I bring him my private thoughts, but the Bible promises us, "Where two or three have gathered together in my name, there I am among them" (Matthew 18:20). That's another reason gathering with other women is such a blessing. We can pray together and talk to God as a group. For many who are used to hearing the pastor pray in church or participating when the congregation prays a printed prayer out loud, praying from our hearts in front of others can be absolutely daunting. Oh, but what a blessing it can be to share with one another our inmost beings! It is so important to make your women's group meetings places where everyone is encouraged, but not compelled, to pray. We want to make each other feel as comfortable approaching our Lord as possible. So, if you are a leader, don't assume others can't pray out loud. If you are not a leader, don't assume you can't lead prayer. If people around you prefer to be quiet, remember that their voices are still part of our prayers and can be heard by God.

Finally, we need to recognize that we can be prayer role models, especially for our children. We can teach each other to pray and assure our children that there is nothing that we can't share with God. There is no concern too big or too small that it cannot be brought to their Savior.

PERSONAL MEDITATION
Do you feel like God hears you when you pray?

When is your favorite time to talk to God?

How do you feel about praying in front of others?

How might more prayer make your life better?

Who needs your prayers right now?

PRAYER SUGGESTIONS

Ask God to show you more opportunities to pray for others.

How amazing it is, Almighty God, that I, who am nothing, can speak to you, who is everything! Thank you for the gift of communicating with you. Help me remember that you are always there and that you are ready to listen. Amen. ⚜

Day 6

QUESTIONS FOR GROUP DISCUSSION

Share with one another some of your thoughts from this week's readings.

Read the book of Ruth again. Take turns reading by verse or by paragraph:

How did Naomi guide Ruth?

Why do you think Ruth had such trust in Naomi's wisdom?

How were Ruth and Naomi rescued?

What brought Naomi from a place of anxiety to a place of confidence?

From where did her confidence originate?

Was Naomi happy?

How can members of your group identify with Naomi?

Consider this passage: "A happy heart makes the face cheerful" (Proverbs 15:13 NIV).

What does it mean to you?

Because this is the last week of this particular Bible study, take this time to talk with your group about your next group adventure. Keep the momentum of studying, worshiping, and sharing God's love together.

PRAYER SUGGESTIONS

By now, hopefully, all of the women in your group might be willing to pray out loud a short prayer from their hearts. Take turns going around the table allowing prayers of thankfulness to be brought to the Lord, but don't make anyone feel ashamed if she just can't pray out loud.

Precious Holy Spirit, thank you for bringing us to faith in your gospel and for strengthening that faith. Christ Jesus, thank you for our gift of salvation through your life, death, and resurrection. Father, thank you for creating our beautiful and special feminine hearts and souls. Lord, we ask you to help us forgive, support, and protect one another and that you would give us opportunities to reach out with your gospel to those around us. We praise you, Triune God, for all that you are and for all your activity on our behalf. Amen. ⚜